MARY BERRY & LUCY YOUNG

At Home

MARY BERRY & LUCY YOUNG

At Home

BOOKS

3 5 7 9 10 8 6 4 2

Published in 2013 by BBC Books, an imprint of Ebury Publishing,
a Random House Group Company. *Mary Berry at Home* was first
published in 1996. This edition is fully revised and updated and
contains 60 new recipes.

Text © Mary Berry 2013
Mary Berry has asserted her right to be identified as the author of this
Work in accordance with the Copyright, Designs and Patents Act 1988.
Photography and design © Woodlands Books Ltd 2013

The Random House Group Limited Reg. No. 954009

Addresses for companies within the Random House Group can
be found at www.randomhouse.co.uk

A CIP catalogue record for this book is available from the British Library.

ISBN 978 1 849 90480 3

The Random House Group Limited supports the Forest Stewardship
Council® (FSC®), the leading international forest-certification organisation.
Our books carrying the FSC label are printed on FSC®-certified paper.
wFSC is the only forest-certification scheme supported by the leading
environmental organisations, including Greenpeace. Our paper procurement
policy can be found at www.randomhouse.co.uk/environment

MIX
Paper from
responsible sources
FSC™ C004592

Commissioning Editor: Muna Reyal
Project Editor: Laura Higginson
Copy Editor: Emily Hatchwell
Design and Art Direction: Smith & Gilmour Ltd
Photographers: Keiko Oikawa & Noel Murphy
Food Stylist: Kim Morphew
Props Stylists: Jo Harris & Lydia Brun
Hair & Makeup: Jo Penford
Production: Helen Everson

Colour origination by AltaImage, London
Printed and bound in Germany by Firmengruppe APPL,
aprinta druck, Wemding

To buy books by your favourite authors and register for offers,
visit www.randomhouse.co.uk

Contents

Introduction

Welcome to this new and updated edition of *At Home!* This recipe collection is full of my favourite recipes – dishes I return to time and time again. There are dishes here that have come about because of a particular occasion, like Flying Fish Pâté (page 17); that have been shared by friends, such as Chicken & Sausage Bacon Bundles (page 69); or have been handed down through the generations, including Granny's Plum Pie (page 184). I've adapted and revised the recipes over the years but they've stood the test of time.

This book contains all the changes I've made to the original *At Home* recipes, plus 60 brand-new recipes. My aim, and that of Lucy Young, my assistant for some 23 years now and my closest friend, is that you will find inspiration and help in this book, whenever you need it and for whatever occasion.

My cooking is divided into two kinds – cooking for family and cooking for guests. For the majority of the time, I cook dishes I know my family love, accompanied by lots of vegetables and fruit. These are often quick dishes or make-ahead recipes and we enjoy the leftovers the next day. I try to keep family cooking balanced, without lots of fat but still include all the foods we love.

When cooking for guests, similar principles must apply – you should always cook what people enjoy, but a little more planning is helpful! The secret of entertaining for me is being able to enjoy the company of your guests, as most of the time I have prepared the majority of the meal ahead. But even for more formal occasions, with some forward planning and sensible menu selections, you can still be part of the fun, even while the food is cooking.

To help with both kinds of occasions, Lucy and I have tried to make the book as easy to use as possible.

The first part of the book is divided into courses – first courses, mains, sides and hot and cold puddings. Then within each of these chapters, there are first simple ideas, which could work well for weeknights or relaxed entertaining, followed by more intricate dishes, which take a little more time, but are my staples for dinner parties and special occasions. Most of the recipes can be easily halved or doubled to suit, but in Chapter 2 there is a section specifically for 'feeding crowds' as well.

Cooking for large numbers (we define this as 8 people or more) is a little different to everyday cooking and, to reduce stress levels, I find one-pot and make-ahead meals the best solution. It's always good to remember that cooking for others doesn't mean pulling out all the stops and cooking the most exotic ingredients you can buy or rushing out to find a new recipe to wow. Cooking doesn't have to be adventurous, but it should always be delicious! The recipes I have included here for large parties have this covered.

We've tried to make Chapter 3 – lots of side dishes – as useful as possible by suggesting other dishes in the book that they would work well with. But our suggestions are by no means exhaustive, so please do mix and match as you please.

In Chapter 4 there are cold desserts and hot puddings as well as some crowd-pleasing big desserts that will again feed 8 people or more. I find Canterbury Tart (page 196) is always a winner, or try Hazelnut Pavlova (page 192) – meringues always look impressive but are so simple to make.

With main meals covered, Chapters 5 and 6 are for the occasions in between – morning coffee, afternoon tea and evening drinks. Turn to Chapter 5 for some of my foolproof bakes, including Buttermilk Sultana Scones and Proper Sandwiches (pages 230 and 234) as well as new dainties such as Mini Victoria Sandwiches and Mini Raspberry Tartlets (pages 238 and 241).

And then Chapter 6 contains my favourite canapés and drinks for parties. Many of these can be made well in advance along with the drinks, so you can enjoy your time with your guests.

When I first sat down to write *At Home*, over 15 years ago, I wanted to provide home cooks with delicious, Cordon Bleu standard recipes made easily. I wanted to cut out all the long processes to provide simple food for busy families, using fresh ingredients rather than packets and convenience foods.

Back then, I noted the change in cooking fashions – stir-fries were becoming increasingly popular and ingredients such as crème fraîche and yoghurt were more readily available in half-fat versions! I remember when a whole roasted chicken was a special Sunday treat and if you wanted chicken pieces, you'd have to joint the chicken yourself. Game is also now much more readily available in butchers and large supermarkets.

Times have, fortunately, continued to change and our diets are so varied now. The range of ingredients sold in super-markets is extraordinary – homecooking has never been easier. All you need is a stock of tried-and-tested, reliable recipes.

So Lucy and I have tried to make this book as helpful as possible – every recipe includes prepare ahead and freezing instructions, and for Aga users (like us) we explain how you can cook every recipe, too. I've included some tips that I find useful throughout. And at the back of the book, you will find some extra information on freezing, using your store cupboard and menu planning among other things, which I hope will help you make the most of your kitchen and time. There are also some homemade stock recipes to try.

When you need inspiration, I hope you will turn to this book. I also hope these recipes will become your family's favourites, as they have been with my children and now my grandchildren.

MARY BERRY

Conversion Tables

Conversions are approximate and have been rounded up or down.
Follow one set of measurements only – do not mix metric and imperial.

MEASUREMENTS

metric	imperial
5mm	¼in
1cm	½in
2.5cm	1in
5cm	2in
7.5cm	3in
10cm	4in
12.5cm	5in
15cm	6in
18cm	7in
20cm	8in
23cm	9in
25cm	10in
30cm	12in

OVEN TEMPERATURES

140°C	Fan 120°C	275°F	Gas 1
150°C	Fan 130°C	300°F	Gas 2
160°C	Fan 140°C	325°F	Gas 3
180°C	Fan 160°C	350°F	Gas 4
190°C	Fan 170°C	375°F	Gas 5
200°C	Fan 180°C	400°F	Gas 6
220°C	Fan 200°C	425°F	Gas 7
230°C	Fan 210°C	450°F	Gas 8
240°C	Fan 220°C	475°F	Gas 9

VOLUME

metric	imperial
25ml	1fl oz
50ml	2fl oz
85ml	3fl oz
100ml	3½fl oz
150ml	5fl oz (¼ pint)
200ml	7fl oz
300ml	10fl oz (½ pint)
450ml	15fl oz (¾ pint)
600ml	1 pint
700ml	1¼ pints
900ml	1½ pints
1 litre	1¾ pints
1.2 litres	2 pints
1.25 litres	2¼ pints
1.5 litres	2½ pints
1.6 litres	2¾ pints
1.75 litres	3 pints
1.8 litres	3¼ pints
2 litres	3½ pints
2.1 litres	3¾ pints
2.25 litres	4 pints
2.75 litres	5 pints
3.4 litres	6 pints
3.9 litres	7 pints
5 litres	8 pints (1 gallon)

WEIGHTS

metric	imperial
15g	½oz
25g	1oz
40g	1½oz
50g	2oz
75g	3oz
100g	4oz
150g	5oz
175g	6oz
200g	7oz
225g	8oz
250g	9oz
275g	10oz
350g	12oz
375g	13oz
400g	14oz
425g	15oz
450g	1lb
550g	1¼lb
675g	1½lb
750g	1¾lb
900g	2lb
1.5kg	3lb
1.75kg	4lb
2.25kg	5lb

Cook's Notes

★ Use this book as a working manual – if you want to add, for example, more basil than I suggest, or try a different kind of cheese or fish, please do so and make a note for next time. By doing this, your cookery book becomes a reliable friend.

★ The recipes are in both metric and imperial measures – pick one or the other and never mix the two.

★ For fan ovens, as a general rule, reduce the temperature by 20 degrees. The recipes have all been tested in my oven but all ovens vary. You might find you need to cook a cake or dish for more or less time than I do. Make a note for the next time. Oven thermometers are useful for getting the correct oven temperature.

★ Defrost frozen dishes thoroughly before reheating, unless the recipe states that you can cook from frozen. Leave plenty of time for defrosting – ideally overnight in the fridge. Take the dish out of the fridge an hour before cooking to allow it to come to room temperature.

★ Most of the recipes in this book call for mild-flavoured sunflower or olive oils. If a specific oil isn't noted, choose your favourite mild-flavoured oil, which won't dominate the dish.

★ There is nothing like real butter, but for baking, baking spreads, which are especially formulated for baking, are perfectly good and less expensive. Just ensure they state that they are suitable for baking. If using real butter for baking, however, it should always be unsalted.

★ Measure ingredients for baking carefully – digital scales are really accurate.

★ I prefer natural sugars, free-range eggs and meat, and sustainably farmed fish, but always buy the best you can afford – it really does pay.

★ Sustainability changes frequently, depending on fish stock levels, so if you find one of the fish used in the book has fallen off the sustainability list ask your fishmonger for an alternative. These days, most large supermarkets have a fish counter and they can advise you.

★ Eggs are large, unless otherwise stated and spoon measures are level.

★ Children, the elderly, pregnant women and anyone in ill-health should avoid recipes containing raw eggs.

FIRST COURSES

*

Relaxed dishes to share
& fancy plates

FIRST COURSES ARE to whet the appetite before the main event, so, the most important thing is to not go mad with portion size! They will also set the tone so choose something that looks as good as it tastes and which complements your main course and dessert.

If you want to wow, why not make your own Gravadlax (page 12) or begin with Seared Tuna with Crunchy Oriental Salad & King Prawns (page 26)? If you want something more low-key, try a sharing plate, such as Tomato, Avocado & Parma Ham Platter (page 16) or a classic Spiced Carrot Soup with Gremolata (page 25). Choose recipes to match the season and weather and go for contrasting textures, colours and ingredients to the following courses to keep your menu interesting.

Whichever type of first-course recipe you choose – relaxed or formal – make sure the following courses won't require you to prepare and cook multiple dishes at once on the night, which is never fun.

There are some storecupboard recipes here too that could be made at a moment's notice – Three-fish Pâté (page 14) uses entirely storecupboard ingredients but tastes fantastic. Pâtés freeze well, because of their high fat content, so they are a great make-ahead starter. Serve your defrosted pâté with homemade bread rolls, refreshed from the freezer, keeping prep time on the day to a minimum. Bruschetta Marinara (page 36) uses a pack of mixed seafood that you can get in most supermarkets, while Warm Chicken Liver Salad with Crisply Fried Sage Leaves (page 29) makes good use of a cheap cut of meat.

And don't forget that two of these first courses would provide a light lunch or supper.

Gravadlax

A classic Scandinavian recipe in which raw salmon is cured for 24 hours in a mixture of salt, pepper and dill and then served with a mustard and dill sauce. It is simplicity itself to prepare, looks imposing on the plate and tastes wonderful. Allow 4–5 slices per portion.

SERVES 12–16

2 sides of salmon, with skin on

3 tablespoons dried dill

3 tablespoons coarse sea salt

1 tablespoon freshly ground black pepper

4 tablespoons caster sugar

For the mustard dill sauce

6 tablespoons Dijon mustard

4 tablespoons caster sugar

2 tablespoons white wine vinegar

2 egg yolks

300ml (10 fl oz) sunflower oil

Salt and freshly ground black pepper

4 tablespoons chopped fresh dill or
   2 tablespoons dried dill

PREPARING AHEAD

Have slices arranged ready on serving plates, covered with clingfilm and chilled. The sauce can be kept in a sealed jar or plastic container in the fridge for a week. The plates can be kept for up to 6 hours.

FREEZING

Wrap each finished gravadlax fillet tightly in clingfilm, seal and label, then freeze for up to 2 months. The sauce is not suitable for freezing. Part-thaw the salmon for 1 hour before slicing.

Sprinkle an equal quantity of dill over each salmon fillet, followed by the salt, then the pepper and finally the sugar. Press these on to the fillets using the flat of your hand, then match the two fillets together, skin-side outside, re-forming the fish. Wrap in clingfilm.

Put the fish inside a large plastic bag, seal, and put the bag on a tray that will fit in the fridge. Check that the fillets are still in position one on top of the other, then put another baking tray on top and firmly weight it with scale weights or tinned foods.

Put the fish into the fridge and leave for about 24 hours, until the salt and sugar have dissolved, turning the fish once and replacing the weighted tray on top. Quite a lot of syrupy liquid will form over this period. Discard all this liquid before moving to the next stage.

To make slicing easier, it is best to partially freeze the fish. Wrap the fillets separately in clingfilm and freeze for 4–6 hours so the fish is firm but still pliable.

Remove one fillet from the freezer, unwrap it, then cut thin slices using a sharp knife angled at about 45 degrees. (This gives the widest possible slices, each with its edge of dill.) Arrange the slices on serving plates.

To make the sauce, use a small balloon whisk to beat together the mustard, sugar, vinegar and egg yolks in a bowl. Gradually beat in the oil a drop at a time until the sauce thickens. Season with salt and pepper and stir in the dill. Spoon a little sauce beside the fillets on each plate and serve the rest separately.

Three-fish Pâté

A recipe that looks almost too unassuming and easy but is worth its weight in gold, this pâté is one of those store-cupboard recipes that can be put together in no time. Served spooned up in a swirl in individual ramekins, it looks – and tastes – as though you have really tried. It is delicious with good-quality brown or walnut bread toast, served hot. Any leftovers make rather superior picnic sandwiches.

SERVES 6

1 × 120g tin sardines in oil
1 × 50g tin anchovies in oil
1 × 185g tin tuna in oil
Juice of 1 lemon
175g (6oz) soft butter
A small handful of fresh parsley sprigs
12 sprigs of fresh dill
Salt and freshly ground black pepper

TIP
If you can't find unwaxed oranges or lemons, wash them in hot water and detergent before using. This gets rid of any wax coating and also helps the fruit give more juice, more freely.

Empty the contents of the tins of sardines and anchovies, including the oil, into a food processor. Discard the oil from the tinned tuna then add to the other fish, followed by the lemon juice, butter, parsley sprigs, half the dill and some pepper.

Process until smooth, then taste and add a little salt if need be. Spoon into a serving dish or individual dishes, cover and put in the fridge until about 2 hours before serving. Remove and leave at room temperature to soften to a spreading consistency.

Garnish with sprigs of fresh dill before serving.

PREPARE AHEAD
Prepare the pâté, cover with clingfilm and keep in the fridge for up to 3 days.

FREEZING
The pâté can be frozen in one large serving dish or individual ones. Cover tightly with foil then seal inside a plastic bag, label, then freeze for up to 1 month.

Med Vegetable Dill Pickle

Serve this pickle as a starter with cold meats or with a cheese board. This (and making gravadlax) is the only time I will use dried herbs as I am not keen unless it is for curing or pickles.

MAKES 2 × 450G (1LB) JARS

1 onion, thinly sliced

1 celery heart stick, thinly sliced

1 yellow pepper, deseeded and cubed

1 red pepper, deseeded and cubed

1 fennel bulb, core removed and cubed

2 small courgettes, sliced

1 cucumber, sliced in half lengthways, seeds removed then sliced

50g (2oz) salt

450g (1lb) caster sugar

300ml (½ pint) white wine vinegar

5 tablespoons water

2 teaspoons mustard seeds

2 teaspoons dried dill

Freshly ground black pepper

Put all the prepared vegetables into a large bowl. Sprinkle over the salt and toss together. Leave for 2–3 hours, stirring from time to time, then pour into a colander, rinse the vegetables in cold water and leave to drain.

Measure the sugar, vinegar and water into a large saucepan. Stir slowly over a gentle heat until the sugar has dissolved, then boil rapidly (without the lid) for 5 minutes.

Add the vegetables and simmer for 5 minutes. Meanwhile, sterilize your jam jars by pouring water just below boiling point into the clean jam jars (or you can sterilize in the dishwasher).

Add the mustard seeds, dill and some black pepper, and stir. Bring to the boil then spoon the vegetables and liquid into clean sterilized jam jars and seal. When cool, label and store in the fridge.

PREPARE AHEAD

The pickle can be made up to 2 weeks ahead. Store in the fridge.

AGA

Cook the vinegar and sugar on the simmering plate, stirring until the sugar has dissolved. Move to the boiling plate and rapidly boil without the lid for 5 minutes. Move the pan back to the simmering plate and add the veg. Cook for a further 5 minutes before adding the spices and returning to the boiling plate to bring to the boil, as above.

CUCUMBER & DILL PICKLE

Top and tail 4 cucumbers and halve them lengthways (do not peel them). Slice them into 3mm thick slices and put them in a bowl sprinkled with 50g (2oz) of salt (make sure each cucumber slice is equally seasoned). Cover and leave for 2 hours, then tip the cucumbers into a colander, rinse well with cold water and leave to drain. Mix 450g (1lb) caster sugar with 300ml (10fl oz) white wine vinegar and 5 tbsp of water in a large saucepan. Heat until the sugar has dissolved, then boil without a lid for 5 minutes. Add the cucumber, 450g (1lb) of thinly sliced onions, and 2 tsps each of mustard seeds and dried dill. Season generously with ground black pepper then bring to the boil. Pack into sterilized jars then seal and store in a cool, dry place for up to 2 months or in the fridge for 6 months.

Tomato, Avocado & Parma Ham Platter

This is an ideal sharing plate, for a first course for a dinner party or at lunchtime. The recipe is ideal for the end of May and through June, when asparagus are in season in the UK and, therefore, full of flavour.

SERVES 6

2 bunches of asparagus
   (approx. 30 thin spears)
4 large beefsteak tomatoes
2 ripe avocados
Juice of 1 lemon
250g Campania buffalo mozzarella
6 slices of Parma ham
Salt and freshly ground black pepper
Parmesan shavings

For the pesto dressing
6 tablespoons olive oil
1½ tablespoons white wine vinegar
1 tablespoon Dijon mustard
2 tablespoons fresh basil pesto
2 teaspoons caster sugar

PREPARE AHEAD
The dish can be assembled up to 6 hours ahead, and dressed just before serving.

AGA
Cook the asparagus on the boiling plate.

Trim the asparagus spears, removing any woody ends. Bring a pan of salted water to the boil and boil the asparagus for 3–4 minutes or until just cooked. Drain and refresh in cold water until stone cold.

Score a tiny cross in the bottom of each tomato. Blanch the whole tomatoes in boiling water for about 40 seconds or until the skins are starting to peel away from the flesh. Remove from the pan and submerge in cold water. Carefully peel off the skins. Cut in half and remove the seeds, then cut the flesh into wedges.

Cut the avocado, remove the stones and skin. Slice into thin slices, then toss in lemon juice.

Mix all the dressing ingredients into a bowl and whisk until combined.

Cut the mozzarella into 12 slices then arrange in rows with the slices of tomato and avocado on a long platter. Season with salt and pepper.

Arrange the asparagus into six equal bundles and lay on top of the salad, followed by a swirl of Parma ham. Just before serving, pour over the dressing and scatter over the Parmesan shavings.

Pass the platter around, so each person can take a bundle of asparagus and some of the salad underneath. You can arrange the dish on six individual plates if you prefer.

Flying Fish Pâté

No, not a mistake – in Barbados this is made with flying fish. Since that is obviously unavailable here, you can use plaice or lemon sole instead. My cousin invented the pâté and it freezes well, too.

MAKES 6 RAMEKINS
A knob of butter, softened
300g (10oz) plaice fillet, with skin on
125g tub full-fat cream cheese
2 tablespoons full-fat mayonnaise
A few drops of Tabasco sauce
1 heaped teaspoon horseradish sauce
    or 1 tablespoon creamed horseradish
2 teaspoons lemon juice
3 anchovies, finely chopped
2 teaspoons capers, finely chopped
1 tablespoon parsley, finely chopped

PREPARE AHEAD
The pâté can be made up
to 2 days ahead.

FREEZE
It freezes well in ramekins.

AGA
Bake the fish in the
simmering oven for
10–12 minutes.

Preheat the oven to 200°C/180°C fan/Gas 6.

Lightly butter a piece of foil then sit the plaice fillet, skin-side up, on top. Wrap the foil around the fish and place on a baking sheet. Bake for 8–10 minutes or until the fish is cooked. Remove the foil, peel off the skin and set aside to cool.

Measure the remaining ingredients together in a bowl and season well. Beat well until smooth. Flake the plaice and add to the bowl. Stir until combined.

Divide the mixture among six small ramekins. Chill for 1 hour before serving the pâté cold with toast.

Butternut Squash & Caramelized Walnut Salad

This salad is best dressed at the last moment; otherwise the leaves will become limp.

SERVES 4

1 medium butternut squash
2 tablespoons olive oil
Salt and freshly ground black pepper
6 rashers of smoked streaky bacon
A knob of butter
50g (2oz) broken pieces of walnuts
2 teaspoons light brown sugar
75g (3oz) rocket leaves
50g (2oz) lamb's lettuce
150g (5oz) feta cheese, crumbled

For the dressing
3 tablespoons olive oil
1½ tablespoons white wine vinegar
1 teaspoon Dijon mustard
1½ teaspoons runny honey

PREPARE AHEAD
The salad can be assembled
up to 4 hours ahead.
Dress just before serving.
Does not freeze.

AGA
Fry the walnuts on the
boiling plate, watching
carefully so that they don't
burn. Roast the squash on
the floor of the roasting oven
for 30 minutes. Add the
bacon 10 minutes before the
end of the roasting time.

Preheat the oven to 220°C/200°C fan/Gas 7.

Peel the squash using a small sharp knife. Remove the seeds and slice into 2cm cubes. Toss in the oil and season then arrange in a single layer on a baking sheet lined with baking parchment. Roast in the oven for 30 minutes until tender and tinged brown.

Put the bacon on a small baking sheet and cook in the oven for about 15 minutes until brown and crisp. Drain on kitchen paper then break into small pieces.

Melt the butter in a small frying pan. Add the walnuts and coat in the butter, then sprinkle over the sugar and fry until the sugar has melted and the nuts are coated. Set aside.

Mix the salad leaves together and arrange in a salad bowl or serving dish. Scatter over the squash, bacon and feta. Mix all of the dressing ingredients together and drizzle over the salad, then sprinkle with the nuts and serve at once.

Roasted Red Pepper Soup

Red peppers are so often only associated with summer cooking, but this is a lovely warming soup for the autumn. For anyone who has never roasted peppers before the process can seem a bit extreme, and in this recipe all the blackened skin actually goes into the soup. Keep going and you will end up with a good, well-rounded flavour. It adapts very happily for vegetarians; simply substitute vegetable stock for the chicken stock.

MAKES 1.75 LITRES
(3 PINTS) TO SERVE 6–8
6 large red peppers
2 tablespoons olive oil
1 large onion, chopped
2 garlic cloves, finely chopped
6 tomatoes, quartered
900ml (1½ pints) Chicken Stock
   (see page 248)
1½ tablespoons balsamic vinegar
1½ tablespoons brown sugar
Salt and freshly ground black pepper

For the garlic croutons
350g (12oz) sliced white bread
5 tablespoons olive oil
3 fat garlic cloves
Salt and freshly ground black pepper
4 tablespoons freshly grated Parmesan

Preheat the oven 220°C/200°C fan/Gas 7.

Slice each pepper in half and remove the stalk and seeds. Place, cut-side down, on a baking sheet. Roast in the oven for 30 minutes until tinged brown.

While the peppers are cooking, heat the oil in a large pan, add the onion and garlic, cover and fry gently until softened but not coloured.

When the peppers are ready, add to the pan along with the tomatoes, stock, balsamic and sugar, and stir. Bring to the boil and simmer for 10–15 minutes or until the onions are completely soft.

Process the soup until smooth. Rinse out the pan, position a large sieve over the top and pour the processed soup into the sieve. Using a rubber spatula, gently stir the purée around to help it through the sieve, but do not actively rub it through. Discard what is left in the sieve.

Taste the soup and season with salt and pepper. You may like to add a little more sugar to the soup and to thin it with a little additional stock or water.

To make the garlic croutons, discard the crusts, then cut the bread into small cubes. Put these in a bowl then sprinkle with the olive oil and garlic and season well with salt and pepper. Use your hands to toss the bread cubes so they are evenly coated in the oil, garlic and seasoning. Leave aside for 10 minutes.

The soup can be made, quickly cooled, then stored in a sealed container in the fridge for up to 48 hours. The croutons can be made up to 2 weeks ahead and stored in an airtight container in the fridge. Reheat in a pan to just below boiling point.

....

FREEZE
Pour the soup into a large freezer container. Cool, seal and label, then freeze for up to 1 month.

....

AGA
Roast the peppers in a foil-lined roasting tin on a rack at the top of the roasting oven for about 30 minutes or until blackened. Bake the croutons on the floor of the roasting oven for 10 minutes.

....

TIP
To freeze stocks and soups, save plastic mineral water bottles and those sturdy cartons that come filled with yoghurt or cream. Wash them thoroughly, then fill to within about 2.5cm (1in) of the top. This allows for the expansion of the liquid when freezing.

Meanwhile, brush a baking tray with a little oil and preheat the grill to maximum. Sprinkle the bread cubes with the Parmesan and toss again. Spread them out in a single layer on the baking tray, then position the tray under the grill. Watch these all the time they are cooking and shake and turn the cubes so they become evenly browned. Cool and serve separately with the hot soup.

Italian Black Olive & Cheese Rolls

A lot of people seem frightened of making bread; don't be. These rolls are delicious and very simple to make. Once you have made them once or twice you will probably feel brave enough to start adding your own flavouring ingredients (see Tip). Look out for Pecorino cheese in your supermarket or delicatessen; it is slightly softer (and often cheaper) than Parmesan, with a salty flavour.

MAKES 12

350g (12oz) strong white flour
1 teaspoon salt
½ packet fast-action dried yeast
Approx. 250ml (8fl oz) warm water
1 tablespoon olive oil
25g (1oz) stoned black olives, chopped
25g (1oz) mature Cheddar,
    freshly grated
25g (1oz) Parmesan or Pecorino,
    freshly grated
Freshly ground black pepper
1 egg, beaten, to glaze

First, grease a baking tray.

Measure the flour into a large bowl, add the salt and yeast, followed by the water and oil, then mix to a pliable dough. It is far better for the dough to be on the wet and sticky side rather than dry.

Turn out on to a lightly floured work surface and knead for about 5 minutes. Alternatively, use a processor or mixer fitted with a dough hook to do the hard work for you. Once the dough leaves the work surface clean and forms a smooth elastic ball, return it to a greased bowl, cover with clingfilm and leave in a warm place to rise for about 2 hours or until doubled in size.

Turn the dough out on to a lightly oiled surface and pat out to a flattened shape. Press the olives, half the cheese and a little freshly ground pepper on to the surface, then gather up the dough and knead briefly to distribute the flavouring ingredients evenly.

Divide the mixture into twelve pieces and form into balls. Arrange them on the baking tray, then brush with beaten egg and sprinkle with the remaining cheese.

PREPARE AHEAD
Seal the cooled rolls inside a
plastic bag and keep for up to
24 hours in the fridge. Refresh
by sprinkling the rolls with a
little water and reheating in a
preheated oven at 180°C/160°C
fan/Gas 4 for about 5–8 minutes.

FREEZE
Seal the cooled rolls inside a
plastic bag and freeze for up
to 3 months.

AGA
Bake on the grid shelf on the
floor of the roasting oven for
about 15 minutes. If the bases
of the rolls are not quite brown,
place the baking sheet on the
floor of the roasting oven for
a further 5 minutes.

TIP
As an alternative, try adding
50g (2oz) of sun-dried tomatoes
in olive oil, drained and chopped,
with 1 teaspoon of dried basil
and a chopped, fried onion,
instead of the olives and cheese.
These tomato rolls are also good
topped with sunflower seeds.

Seal the tray inside a large plastic bag,
trapping a fair amount of air in the bag so
it puffs up well above the dough and is not
in contact with it. Leave to rise in a warm
place for about 30 minutes until the rolls
have doubled in size.

Preheat the oven to 200°C/180°C fan/Gas 6.

Bake the rolls for 15–20 minutes or until
a good crusty, golden brown. Cool on a wire
rack and try not to eat them until they are
at least warm!

Soupe Grandmère

This is a great family recipe. A robust, no-nonsense, home-made soup, served with Parmesan and a warm, grainy, brown bread. It is the sort of soup that is best made in large quantities, so people can have seconds and still leave enough for the following day.

MAKES 3.4 LITRES (6 PINTS)
TO SERVE 12

25g (1oz) butter

1 large onion, finely chopped

3 carrots, diced

2 celery sticks, finely chopped

1 leek, thinly sliced

1 tablespoon plain flour

2.75 litres (5 pints) Chicken Stock
(see page 248) or make using
chicken stock cubes

4 tablespoons tomato purée

50g (2oz) spaghetti, broken into
short lengths

¼ small head of cabbage,
very finely shredded

Salt and freshly ground black pepper

To serve
Freshly grated Parmesan

TIP
I believe in adding a little flour to thicken soups, so all the ingredients remain evenly distributed, even after standing in the fridge.

Heat the butter in a large, deep pan and fry the onion for 5–8 minutes over a moderate heat until it begins to soften and colour. Add the carrots, celery and leek and fry gently for 8–10 minutes, stirring frequently. Sprinkle in the flour, stir it in and cook for 2 minutes.

Gradually add the stock and tomato purée, stirring all the while. Bring to the boil then cover, lower the heat and continue to simmer gently for 30 minutes or until all the vegetables are tender.

Add the spaghetti and cabbage and continue to cook, without the lid, on the hob for a further 10 minutes. Taste and season carefully with salt and pepper.

Serve in deep soup bowls accompanied by plenty of freshly grated Parmesan.

PREPARE AHEAD
The soup can be made, quickly cooled, then stored in the fridge for up to 2 days. Reheat in a pan to just below boiling point.

FREEZE
Pour the soup into a large freezer container. Cool, seal and label, then freeze for up to 1 month.

AGA
Make on the boiling plate. After adding the liquid, bring to the boil, cover and transfer to the simmering oven for 40 minutes or until the vegetables are tender. Remove from the simmering oven and add the spaghetti and cabbage. Cook for a further 10 minutes on the boiling plate, or until the spaghetti is cooked.

Spiced Carrot Soup with Gremolata

Gremolata is an aromatic mixture of parsley, grated lemon zest and garlic which gives an excellent, fresh-tasting lift to all manner of soups and stews when added at the last moment. Taste the soup carefully before serving: the season of the year will affect the flavour of carrots, so the quantities of sugar and lemon might need to be adjusted a little.

SERVES 6–8

3 tablespoons sunflower oil

2 onions, coarsely chopped

2 teaspoons ground coriander

1 teaspoon garam masala

¼ teaspoon hot Madras curry powder

1 teaspoon peeled and grated
fresh ginger root

1 tablespoon plain flour

900g (2lb) carrots, thickly sliced

1.5 litres (2½ pints) Chicken Stock
(see page 248)

Juice of 1 lemon

1 teaspoon sugar

Salt and freshly ground black pepper

For the gremolata

A generous handful of fresh parsley

Grated zest of 1 lemon

1 fat garlic clove, crushed

Measure the oil into a large, deep pan and heat gently. Stir in the onions and cook over a low heat for about 15 minutes or until the onions are softened but not coloured.

While the onions are cooking, measure the dry spices and ginger on to a plate with the flour. When the onions are ready, stir in the flour and spices and cook for 2 minutes.

Add the carrots, pour in the stock and bring to the boil. Adjust the heat to a gentle simmer, cover and cook for 10 minutes. Remove the pan from the heat and leave to cool.

Add the lemon juice and sugar. Pour the soup into a sieve then tip the vegetables into a food processor. Process the vegetables until you have a smooth purée. Rinse out the pan.

Return both the liquid and the vegetable purée to the rinsed-out pan and reheat. Taste and season with salt and pepper, adding a little more lemon juice or sugar if you prefer.

To prepare the gremolata, first discard all the parsley stalks, then make sure that the leaves are completely dry. Combine the leaves with the grated lemon zest and garlic and chop very finely. Serve the soup with a little of the gremolata sprinkled over each bowl.

PREPARE AHEAD
The soup can be made, quickly cooled, then stored in a sealed container in the fridge for up to 2 days. Reheat in a pan to just below boiling point. Make the gremolata when needed.

FREEZE
Pour the soup into a large freezer container. Cool, seal and label, then freeze for up to 1 month.

AGA
Sauté the onions on the boiling plate for 1 minute, then cover and transfer to the simmering oven for 15 minutes or until tender. Stir in the rest of the ingredients, cover and return to the simmering oven for 20 minutes or until tender.

Seared Tuna with Crunchy Oriental Salad & King Prawns

For a smart healthy first course, this is your recipe. Teriyaki sauce can be bought in a bottle, in supermarkets as you would buy soy sauce.

SERVES 6

350g (12oz) thick slice of fresh tuna
8 tablespoons teriyaki sauce
25g (1oz) sesame seeds
Salt and freshly ground black pepper
3 tablespoons olive oil
12 large king prawns, shell on

For the salad

1 medium carrot, peeled and sliced
    into matchstick-thin strips
3 spring onions, sliced into
    matchstick-thin strips
1 Little Gem lettuce, thinly shredded
25g (1oz) beansprouts

For the dressing

2 tablespoons olive oil
2 tablespoons rice wine or
    white wine vinegar
1½ tablespoons sweet chilli dipping sauce
1 teaspoon finely grated fresh ginger root
1 teaspoon lime juice
A dash of caster sugar

PREPARE AHEAD
The dish can be assembled up
to 6 hours ahead and kept in the
fridge – pour over the dressing
just before serving.

First, prepare the tuna. Using a sharp knife, slice the fish into 3 × 8 × 3cm (1½ × 3 × 1½ in) strips. Measure 2 tablespoons of the teriyaki sauce into a small bowl, add the tuna strips and mix to coat. Marinate in the fridge to for 1 hour.

Scatter the sesame seeds on to a board. Season each strip of tuna and press into the sesame seeds so each slice is coated in seeds.

Heat the oil in a frying pan and flash-fry the tuna for 15–20 seconds on each side until the seeds are lightly golden and the tuna is just starting to cook. Transfer to a plate to rest.

Tip the sliced carrot and spring onions into a bowl of ice cold water and leave for the carrot to crispen and the spring onions to curl.

Measure all the ingredients for the dressing into a bowl and whisk to combine. Season with salt and pepper. Peel the body shell away from the prawns, leaving the head on.

Drain the vegetables from the water and pat dry with kitchen paper. Mix with the lettuce and beansprouts. Take six small plates and divide the vegetables between the plates, arranging a pile just off centre. Place two prawns on each plate next to the salad.

Slice each rectangle of tuna into six and place three slices on each plate next to the prawns. Drizzle a little dressing over the prawns and pour the remainder over the crunchy salad.

Take six small ramekins or pots and pour a tablespoon of teriyaki into each. Place a pot on each plate next to the tuna. Serve cold.

Grapefruit & Parma Ham Salad

A very pretty and refreshing first course. It's very quick to put together, especially if you peel and segment the grapefruit ahead.

SERVES 6

3 pink grapefruit
2 handfuls of lamb's lettuce
10 radishes, thinly sliced
12 slices of Parma ham
2 teaspoons capers, rinsed and dried
1–2 teaspoons olive oil
Freshly ground black pepper
½ teaspoon sugar

PREPARE AHEAD
The plates can be arranged up to 6 hours ahead, dress just before serving.

Peel and segment the grapefruit over a bowl to catch the juice.

Divide the lamb's lettuce among six plates. Place the grapefruit segments and radish slices on and around the lettuce.

Scrunch up the ham and place two pieces on each plate. Sprinkle with the capers.

Whisk 1–2 teaspoons of grapefruit juice with the oil, black pepper and sugar. Taste and add more oil or fruit juice to taste.

Drizzle a little over each salad and serve at once.

Warm Chicken Liver Salad with Crisply Fried Sage Leaves

If you can, get fresh chicken livers from the butcher. If not, frozen chicken livers are available in most super-markets. Thawing them overnight in the fridge is best. Drain and dry the livers thoroughly before you fry them, so they can then be seared briefly in a very hot pan and emerge tinged pink and tender.

SERVES 6 AS A FIRST COURSE OR 4 FOR A LIGHT LUNCH

450g (1lb) chicken livers

½ crisp lettuce or 2 small round lettuces

1 bunch of watercress

3 tablespoons sunflower oil

Approx. 12 large sage leaves

175g (6oz) thick slices of streaky bacon, cut into thin strips

3 × 1cm (½in) thick slices wholemeal bread, crusts removed and cubed

4 tablespoons French Dressing (see page 148), made with wholegrain mustard

25g (1oz) butter

1 tablespoon balsamic vinegar

Salt and freshly ground black pepper

PREPARE AHEAD
Fry the sage leaves, drain and leave aside. Fry the bacon strips and bread cubes. At this stage the recipe can be left for up to 6 hours.

FREEZE
You can use croutons that you have frozen earlier. Just add them to the pan for 1–2 minutes once the bacon has become crisp.

Put the chicken livers to drain in a sieve over a bowl. Using a pair of kitchen scissors, cut the larger pieces of liver in half and remove any stringy bits. Transfer the prepared livers to a double thickness of kitchen paper to absorb any remaining juices.

Tear the lettuce leaves into pieces and discard any large watercress stalks. Divide the leaves among six serving plates, cover with clingfilm and chill in the fridge until ready to serve.

Heat the oil in a large frying pan until very hot. Fry a few sage leaves at a time for a few seconds only. The leaves should turn a darker green, but not brown. Lift them carefully from the pan with a fork and leave aside to drain on kitchen paper.

Now add the bacon strips to the pan and, when they start to brown, stir in the bread cubes. Fry together until crisp and brown, then drain on kitchen paper.

Remove the salads from the fridge and dress. Reheat the oil in the pan and let it get very hot before adding the butter. As soon as the foam subsides, put the chicken livers into the pan. Sauté for up to 3 minutes over a high heat, then pull the pan aside, add the vinegar and season with salt and pepper.

Swirl the livers in the pan juices, then spoon the contents over the salads. Quickly sprinkle with the bacon and croutons and top with the fried sage leaves. Serve immediately.

Duck Terrine with Orange Confit

I first tried the original recipe for this at a friend's supper party and thought it was so delicious, I had to create my own version. An unusual combination of duck, pork, orange and pistachio nuts, this dish is straightforward to make and can be prepared several days ahead along with the orange confit.

SERVES 8–10 AS
A FIRST COURSE OR
6–8 AS A MAIN COURSE

3 large bay leaves
Approx. 8 long, thin rashers of streaky
   bacon, rind removed
2 large garlic cloves, chopped
450g (1lb) minced pork
Approx. 1½ teaspoons salt
Freshly ground black pepper
Grated zest and juice of 1 large orange
2 tablespoons dry vermouth
   or white wine
150g (5oz) fresh white breadcrumbs
100g (4oz) shelled, unsalted
   pistachio nuts
2 large duck breasts

To serve
Orange Confit (see page 33)

Preheat the oven to 200°C/180° fan/Gas 6. Grease a non-stick loaf tin measuring 23 × 11.5cm (9 × 4½ in).

Lay the bay leaves down the centre of the loaf tin.

With the flat side of a kitchen knife, spread and stretch out each bacon slice thinly on a board, then arrange so they overlap across the length of the loaf tin, on top of the bay leaves. Any surplus bacon can be left hanging over the edge of the tin as this can be folded in over the meat mixture when the tin is full. Cut a bacon slice into three to line each short end of the tin.

Whizz the garlic briefly, then add the pork and process for a further 20 seconds. Do this in batches if necessary. Add the salt, a generous amount of pepper, the orange zest and juice, the vermouth or wine and the breadcrumbs. Whizz again, just enough to mix together thoroughly.

Press half the mixture into the lined tin, level with the back of a spoon then sprinkle in half the pistachio nuts.

Skin the duck breasts, reserving the skin, then cut the meat into 5mm (¼-in) strips down the length of the breasts and arrange these lengthways in the tin.

Season well with salt and pepper before sprinkling in the remaining nuts. Press the remaining meat mixture on top, level, and fold the bacon strips in over the meat. Cover the meat with the skins from the duck breasts to keep the terrine moist.

PREPARE AHEAD
The covered, weighted terrine
can be kept in the fridge for up
to 1 week.

FREEZE
Not recommended, but if you
must, 2 weeks only.

AGA
Cook the terrine for 1¼ hours
in the roasting tin half-filled
with boiling water, as above,
on the grid shelf on the floor of
the roasting oven with the cold
plain shelf on the second set
of runners.

Cover with foil, then put the tin in a small
roasting tin on the centre shelf of the oven.
Carefully pour in sufficient boiling water
to come half-way up the side of the loaf tin.

Bake for 1¼ hours, then remove the foil
and discard the duck skin. To make sure
the terrine is cooked, insert a thin skewer
in the centre. When the skewer is removed
the juices should flow clear; if not, bake for
a further 15 minutes. Remove the loaf tin
from the water bath and leave to cool for
about 2 hours.

When the terrine is cold, cover the surface
with a sheet of clingfilm and put a matching
size loaf tin on top. Put weights inside the
second loaf tin and put the whole thing in
a dish to catch any juices. Transfer to the
fridge for 24–48 hours to become firm.

To turn out the terrine, run a knife around
the edge to loosen the meat from the sides
of the tin. Position a serving plate on top
and invert so the tin can be lifted free of
the terrine. Only dip the tin in hot water
if the terrine will not come out of the tin.

Orange Confit

This is delicious served with the Duck Terrine or with cooked cold meats at Christmas. Make the confit ahead of time since it is best kept in the fridge for 3 weeks before eating. Once opened, use it within 5 days.

FILLS 1 × 500ML (17FL OZ) JAR

3 seedless oranges
85ml (3fl oz) white wine
    or cider vinegar
225g (8oz) sugar
4 cloves
1 teaspoon allspice berries
1 × 7.5cm (3in) cinnamon stick

AGA
Put the sliced oranges in a pan with just sufficient water to cover. Bring to simmering point then cover and transfer to the floor of the simmering oven for about 1 hour or until the rind is tender. Cook the slices in the spiced vinegar, uncovered, on the floor of the simmering oven for about 30 minutes. Use a slotted spoon to transfer the orange slices to a preserving jar. Boil the remaining pan juices for 5–10 minutes or until the juice has become syrupy, then pour over the fruit. There should be just sufficient liquid to cover the fruit.

Scrub the oranges with a brush in warm, soapy water. Using a very sharp knife, slice each one into 5mm (¼-in) slices, discarding the ends.

Lay the slices flat in a medium-sized pan and add just sufficient cold water to cover. Bring to simmering point, then cover and continue to cook very gently for about 1 hour or until the rind is tender. Use a slotted spoon to transfer the slices to a bowl, then discard the liquid left in the pan.

Measure the vinegar, sugar and spices into the same pan and warm over a low heat until the sugar has dissolved. Return the orange slices to the pan and bring to the boil.

Tilt a lid over the top of the pan and boil gently until the juices take on a slightly caramelised appearance and the orange slices are translucent. Spoon into a hot, sterilized preserving jar. Cover and leave to cool. Seal, label and keep in the fridge for 3 weeks before using.

Goat's Cheese Crostini with Caramelized Onion Salad

This cold salad with warm crostini is a perfect prepare-ahead recipe, and great for vegetarians. The peppers can be found in the deli area of the supermarket, already chargrilled and ready to eat.

SERVES 6

Olive oil

1 red onion, thinly sliced

1 tablespoon brown sugar

1 tablespoon balsamic vinegar

100g (4oz) ciabatta bread

225g (8oz) goat's cheese in a roll

Lamb's lettuce and pea shoots

175g (6oz) chargrilled peppers,
   thinly sliced

Salad dressing of your choice

Salt and freshly ground
   black pepper

PREPARE AHEAD
The crostini can be toasted
and topped with the cheese
up to 6 hours ahead, ready
to cook under the grill
before serving.

AGA
Cook the crostini on the
floor of the roasting oven
for 4 minutes until golden.
Slide on to the top set of
runners in the roasting
oven with the goat's cheese
on top for about 5 minutes.

Heat 1 tablespoon of oil in a frying pan, add the onions and fry for 10 minutes until nearly soft. Add the sugar and vinegar and fry again until glazed and sticky. Set aside to cool.

Preheat the grill. Slice the bread into six fairly thin slices. Lay on a piece of foil in a grill pan. Brush the upper side of the bread with olive oil and grill for a couple of minutes until golden brown then remove the grill.

Cut the goat's cheese into six slices (leaving the skin on) and lay one slice on the untoasted side of each piece of bread. Return the crostini to the grill and grill for few minutes until the cheese is just starting to melt.

Meanwhile, divide the lettuce among six individual plates, and scatter over the sliced peppers and caramelized onion.

Dress the salad with salad dressing and season with salt and pepper. Lay the crostini on top of the salad and serve immediately.

Bruschetta Marinara

Frozen packs of mixed seafood are ideal for this recipe, unless you would rather make up the quantity of shellfish according to your own preferences. This dish takes scarcely 25 minutes to make.

SERVES 6

For the toasts

6 × 1cm (½-in) thick slices of baguette, cut at an oblique angle
3 tablespoons olive oil
1 garlic clove, crushed
2 tablespoons chopped fresh parsley
Salt and freshly ground black pepper

For the seafood sauce

1 tablespoon olive oil
1 onion, finely chopped
1 large garlic clove, crushed
50g (2oz) button mushrooms, coarsely chopped
450g (1lb) frozen mixed seafood, such as prawns, scallops, mussels and squid, thawed and drained
300ml (10fl oz) double cream
2 tablespoons lemon juice
Salt and freshly ground black pepper

To garnish

6 sprigs of fresh parsley
6 lemon wedges

Preheat the oven to 220°C/200°C fan/Gas 7.

First make the toasts. Line a baking tray with foil and arrange the bread slices on top in a single layer. Drizzle with 1 tablespoon of the oil, then turn the slices over, oil-side down. Mix the rest of the oil with the garlic, parsley and some salt and pepper and spread on the other surface of the bread.

Bake for 5–7 minutes or until the bread is browned and crisp then remove from the oven.

To make the seafood sauce, heat the oil in a medium-sized frying pan and fry the onion and garlic for 5–8 minutes over a low to moderate heat until softened and lightly coloured. Add the mushrooms and cook for a further 1–2 minutes.

Add the seafood and allow to heat for a further 2–3 minutes. Stir in the cream, bring to a gentle simmer and continue to cook for 2–3 minutes until everything is tender and the cream has reduced to a sauce consistency.

Remove the pan from the heat, stir in the lemon juice, taste and season with salt and pepper.

Arrange the toasts on warm serving plate(s) and spoon the seafood mixture on to each one. Quickly garnish with sprigs of parsley and lemon wedges and serve hot.

PREPARE AHEAD
Have the toasts ready-made but not spread with garlic and parsley. The seafood mixture can be made, quickly cooled and stored in a covered container in the fridge for up to 6 hours. Then follow the recipe.

AGA
Bake the toasts on a baking tray on the floor of the roasting oven until brown, about 5 minutes, but keep an eye on them. Keep warm in the simmering oven.

Garlic Mushroom Stacks

This makes a delicious and unusual starter and is ideal as a supper dish for vegetarians, served with fresh bread to mop up the juices. Use the recipe to take full advantage of some of the wonderful mixtures of mushrooms some supermarkets sell in a single pack.

SERVES 4

4 flat mushrooms, approx. 10cm (4 in)
   in diameter
Approx. 2 tablespoons olive oil
Salt and freshly ground black pepper
15g (½oz) butter
1 shallot, finely chopped
1 garlic clove, finely chopped
100g (4oz) shiitake mushrooms, sliced
100g (4oz) oyster mushrooms, sliced
100g (4oz) chestnut mushrooms, quartered
1 × 200ml carton full-fat crème fraîche
Juice of ½ lemon
1 tablespoon chopped fresh parsley

To serve
Good brown bread or walnut bread

PREPARE AHEAD
Arrange the fried flat mushrooms in a baking dish, cover and put in the fridge. Cook the other mushrooms completely, cover and put in the fridge. Keep for up to 24 hours. When it's time, pile the mushrooms in cream on to the flat mushrooms, stirring in any juice that might have run out of the caps. Reheat for about 10 minutes in a preheated oven at 220°C/200°C fan/Gas 7. Sprinkle with the parsley.

Preheat the oven to 180°C/160°C fan/Gas 4. You will need a shallow, ovenproof baking dish, just large enough to hold the mushrooms in a single layer.

Twist the central stalks from the flat mushrooms, slice the stalks and reserve. Wipe the caps with kitchen paper.

Heat the olive oil in a frying pan and fry the mushroom caps for 5 minutes, turning them over halfway through the cooking time. Place them in the baking dish, season with salt and pepper, then put in the oven.

Add the butter to the pan, stir in the shallot and cook over a moderate heat for 3 minutes or until the shallot begins to soften and colour. Add the garlic and continue cooking for 1 minute. Add the shiitake, oyster and chestnut mushrooms, the sliced mushroom stalks then the crème fraîche.

Turn down the heat to low and cook gently for about 5 minutes, then uncover and continue to cook until the mushrooms are tender and the sauce has reduced to a nice coating consistency. Add the lemon juice and season to taste. Remove the pan from the heat.

Spoon an equal amount of the mushrooms and sauce over each flat mushroom, sprinkle with parsley and serve with toasted brown bread or walnut bread.

AGA
Prepare following the recipe above, cooking the mushrooms on the boiling plate, then reheat in the roasting oven for about 10 minutes. Serve sprinkled with parsley.

THE
CENTRE
ATTRACTION

*

Family food, special suppers
& suppers for crowds

THIS CHAPTER BEGINS with some family favourites that everyone will enjoy, that don't cost much to make and use only a few utensils, including Quick Chicken Curry (page 48), Really Posh Cottage Pie (page 52) and Whole Roasted Garlic Chicken (page 40). Serve these dishes with green vegetables for a complete meal.

Next come some suggestions for entertaining friends, which are still straightforward to prepare but might use more 'special' ingredients or require a little more effort – Pappardelle with Tomato & Vodka Sauce (page 78), Chicken Breasts with Madeira & Tarragon Sauce (page 80) and Butterflied Lamb in Lemon Marinade (page 76) have always been winners for me.

The butterflied lamb is also one of those dishes that tastes delicious on the barbecue. A few years ago I cooked a charity barbecue and served ten butterflied legs of lamb to 100 guests, accompanied by Roasted Mediterranean Vegetables (page 145), which I made in batches two days before and stored in a new bucket in the fridge – it kept really well!

There are a few recipes in this chapter that can be cooked in the oven or over hot coals, depending on the weather, and we have included both cooking instructions.

The thing to remember about entertaining, is that it doesn't always have to be expensive. Mediterranean Tuna en Croûte (page 124) is the perfect example of a great party recipe done cheaply. It was a recipe that Lucy invented back when she and her friends loved to throw dinner parties but were a bit more hard up! This dish is full of flavour and has real style but costs virtually nothing to make.

Whole Roasted Garlic Chicken

If you have any lemon shells left over after using their juice for another recipe, use these instead of the fresh lemon wedges. Buy the best chicken you can afford for this recipe.

SERVES 6

1 × 1.75kg (4lb) chicken
1 lemon, cut into 6 wedges
A good sprig of fresh thyme

For the garlic butter
2 fat garlic cloves, finely chopped
50g (2oz) butter, at spreading consistency
Salt and freshly ground black pepper

For the vegetables
250g (9oz) shallots, peeled
350g small carrots
3 parsnips, peeled and sliced into thick slices
2 tablespoons olive oil

For the gravy
1 tablespoon plain flour
100ml white wine
400ml (14fl oz) Chicken Stock (see page 248)

To garnish
A small handful of fresh parsley sprigs

PREPARE AHEAD
Cover the prepared chicken with clingfilm. Pile the prepared vegetables in a bowl and cover. Both can be kept in the fridge for up to 24 hours. However, remember that the longer the chicken is kept before cooking, the more the garlic flavour will develop. Make sure that the chicken is at room temperature before roasting.

Preheat the oven to 200°C/180°C fan/Gas 6. You will need a large roasting tin for the chicken, large enough to hold the vegetables in a single layer, as well as the chicken.

Loosen the skin from the neck end of the chicken over the breasts – use your finger to free the skin from the flesh.

Mix the butter and garlic together and season with salt and pepper. Spread the garlic butter under the skin over the breasts.

Stuff the cavity with the lemon wedges and thyme sprigs then place the chicken in a roasting tin. Season with salt and pepper and roast for about 20 minutes.

Toss the prepared vegetables in oil and season with salt and pepper. Scatter the vegetables around the chicken in the roasting tin. Return to the oven for 1 hour or until the vegetables are golden and the chicken is tender, basting from time to time with the juices.

Transfer the chicken to a carving board to rest and spoon the vegetables into a dish and keep warm. Sit the roasting tin on a low heat on the hob, sprinkle in the flour and whisk, scraping up the sides of the tin. Blend in the wine and stock with the whisk and bring to the boil, stirring until thickened.

Carve or joint the chicken and serve with the vegetables and gravy, garnished with parsley.

AGA
Follow the recipe and roast in the roasting oven for about 20 minutes; add the veg and cook for a further 50 minutes.

Chinese Noodles with Sugar Snap Peas

This is ideal for a family supper or interesting lunch. The colour is wonderful and it is a complete meal that needs no extras.

SERVES 6

200g (7oz) Chinese medium
   egg noodles

3 tablespoons sesame or olive oil

350g (12oz) pork fillet, cut into thin strips

2 tablespoons runny honey

1 large, mild onion, thinly sliced

2 garlic cloves, crushed

2.5cm (1in) fresh ginger root,
   peeled and finely grated

1 small red chilli, deseeded and
   finely chopped

2 small red peppers, deseeded and
   thinly sliced

5 spring onions, diagonally sliced

225g (8oz) sugar snap peas

150g (5oz) beansprouts

For the sauce

2 teaspoons cornflour

250ml (8fl oz) Chicken Stock
   (see page 248)

2 tablespoons soy sauce

Salt and freshly ground pepper

PREPARE AHEAD
This recipe is so quick to do
– just have all the ingredients
ready and prepared. The pork
can be browned up to 2 hours
ahead of cooking.

Bring a large pan of well-salted water to the boil. Cook the noodles according to the packet instructions then drain. Using scissors, snip the noodles in half (this makes them easier to handle when eating).

Measure about 2 tablespoons of the oil into a large frying pan. Stir-fry the pork and honey over a high heat for 2–3 minutes until browned but a little under-done. Remove with a slotted spoon and set aside.

Add 1 tablespoon of oil into the pan. Stir in the onion and fry for a few minutes, then add the garlic, ginger, and chilli and stir-fry over a high heat for a few minutes more. Add the peppers, spring onions and sugar snap peas. Continue to stir-fry for 4–5 minutes, adding more oil if needed.

In a small bowl, stir together the cornflour and a little cold stock, then add to the pan, stirring briskly. Bring to the boil and then simmer, returning the pork to the pan to heat through.

Add the drained noodles, then taste and season with soy sauce, and a little salt and black pepper. Add the beansprouts and serve immediately.

Spiced Pork Chops with Mango

....

This is inspired by a recipe in a book by Carole Rymer, a friend and great expert in pig farming. Serve it with rice and a tomato and onion salad scattered with a liberal amount of coarsely chopped fresh parsley or freshly sliced ripe avocado slices.

SERVES 6

3 tablespoons olive oil

175g (6oz) onions, coarsely chopped

2 garlic cloves, crushed

1 tablespoon plain flour

1 tablespoon garam masala

300ml (1fl oz) Chicken Stock
    (see page 248)

50g (2oz) creamed coconut,
    cut into small chunks

Juice of ½ lemon

3 tablespoons mango chutney

Salt and freshly ground black pepper

6 loin pork chops, boned

To make the sauce, add 2 tablespoons of the oil to a frying pan and fry the onions for a few minutes. Add the garlic and fry for 1 minute, then cover, lower the heat and simmer for 15 minutes until soft.

Remove the lid, increase the heat and sprinkle over the flour and garam masala. Stir, then gradually add the stock, creamed coconut, lemon juice and mango chutney. Check the seasoning and set aside.

Heat the remaining oil in a frying pan and fry the chops for 4 minutes on each side.

Reheat the sauce and serve on top of the chops.

....

PREPARE AHEAD
The sauce can be made up to 6 hours ahead.

....

AGA
Start the sauce on the boiling plate, cover and transfer the onions and garlic to the simmering oven for 15 minutes. Continue on the boiling plate. Cook the chops on the boiling plate.

Minted Lamb Casserole with Porcini Mushrooms

A casserole full of flavour and perfect for preparing ahead – one of my favourite lamb casseroles. Serve with mash and vegetables.

SERVES 6

30g dried porcini mushrooms
2 tablespoons olive oil
900g (2lb) lamb neck fillet, cubed
1 large onion, sliced
2 garlic cloves, crushed
25g (1oz) plain flour
300ml (½ pint) red wine
150ml (5fl oz) Chicken Stock
   (see page 248)
1 tablespoon Worcestershire sauce
2–3 tablespoons mint jelly
250g brown chestnut mushrooms,
   halved

PREPARE AHEAD
The casserole can be made up to a day ahead and reheated.

FREEZE
It freezes well, cooked without the mushrooms. Add the mushroom when reheating, to serve.

AGA
Bring to the boil on the boiling plate, cover and transfer to the simmering oven for 1½–2 hours.

Preheat the oven to 160°C/140°C fan/Gas 3.

First, soak the dried mushrooms: place them in a small bowl, pour over 150ml boiling water and leave to soak for 30 minutes. Strain through a sieve, reserving the liquid, and chop the mushrooms fairly finely.

Heat 1 tablespoon of olive oil in a frying pan. Brown the lamb until golden and sealed all over – you may need to do this in batches. Remove with a slotted spoon and set aside.

Heat the remaining oil in the pan, add the onion and garlic and fry for a few minutes.

Measure the flour into a small bowl, whisk in a little red wine until smooth and blended and then pour in the remaining wine. Add this mixture to the pan followed by the stock, Worcestershire sauce, mint jelly, chopped soaked mushrooms and reserved mushroom liquid. Stir and bring to the boil.

Return the lamb to the pan, cover and cook in the oven for 1½ hours or until the lamb is tender. Add the chestnut mushrooms 15 minutes before the end of cooking.

Spicy Pork Meatballs with Noodles

A most successful supper dish that can be prepared ahead. Passata can now be bought in bottles or cartons in most supermarkets.

SERVES 4 (3 BALLS EACH)
2 tablespoons sunflower oil, for frying
Plain flour, for coating
1 × 275g packet medium Chinese egg noodles

For the meatballs
450g (1lb) minced pork
3 garlic cloves, crushed
1 fresh chilli, deseeded and finely chopped
2 teaspoons garam masala
3 tablespoons chopped fresh coriander
1 tablespoon dark soy sauce
1 tablespoon vegetable oil

For the tomato sauce
2 tablespoons vegetable oil
1 onion, very finely chopped
1 fat garlic clove, crushed
600ml (1 pint) passata
2 teaspoons sugar
Salt and freshly ground black pepper
A dash of Tabasco sauce (optional)

To garnish
4 tablespoons chopped fresh coriander

PREPARE AHEAD
The meatballs can be cooked in the sauce, quickly cooled, then covered and stored in the fridge for up to 3 days. Reheat, covered, in a frying pan while the noodles boil.

Combine all the ingredients for the meatballs together in a bowl and mix well. Divide the mixture into 12 pieces and form into balls.

Heat the 2 tablespoons of oil in a large frying pan. Lightly flour the meatballs, then toss straight into the pan and swirl in the hot oil. Cook over a low to moderate heat for 7 minutes or until browned. Use a slotted spoon to remove on to kitchen paper to drain.

To make the tomato sauce, add the further 2 tablespoons of oil to the pan and stir in the onion and garlic. Cover and cook over a low heat for about 15 minutes or until softened and lightly coloured. Add the passata and sugar and season with salt and pepper.

Return the meatballs to the pan. Bring to simmering point, then cover and cook for about 15 minutes.

Meanwhile, cook the noodles in boiling salted water according to the instructions on the packet. When ready, drain and put into a warmed serving dish.

Uncover the pan with the meatballs and continue to cook and reduce if the sauce is a little thin. Taste and season with salt and pepper, adding a dash of Tabasco, if liked. Pour the contents of the pan over the noodles and sprinkle thickly with additional coriander. Serve at once.

FREEZE
Cook the meatballs in the sauce for 15 minutes, then cool quickly and transfer to a freezer container. Freeze for up to 4 months.

Paprika Chicken

A quick and easy supper dish for the family, but certainly distinguished enough to serve for a dinner party. If you prefer to cut the calories, substitute chicken stock for half the crème fraîche and thicken the sauce with 1 teaspoon of cornflour; gently boil the sauce for 2–3 minutes before pouring over the chicken.

SERVES 6
50g (2oz) butter
1 mild onion, thinly sliced
6 chicken breasts, without skin or bone
Salt and freshly ground black pepper
2 good tablespoons mild paprika
1 × 200g carton full-fat crème fraîche

To garnish
2 tablespoons chopped fresh parsley

PREPARE AHEAD
When the chicken and onions have been pan-fried, the pan deglazed and the sauce poured over, cover with foil, cool quickly and keep in the fridge for up to 24 hours. To reheat, bake the foil-covered chicken in the preheated oven as above for about 20 minutes. Expect some fat to come out of the dish when thawed and reheated; just mop it up with kitchen paper.

AGA
Cook on the grid shelf on the floor of the roasting oven for about 20 minutes.

Preheat the oven to 200°C/180°C fan/Gas 6. You will need a shallow ovenproof dish large enough to hold the chicken in one layer.

Heat half the butter in a large frying pan. As soon as the foam starts to subside, stir in the onion, then cover and cook over a low heat for about 10 minutes, or until softened but not coloured. Spread the onion in the base of the ovenproof dish.

Melt the remaining butter in the pan. Season the chicken breasts with salt and pepper, then add to the pan, turning each one to coat it in the hot butter. Brown over a moderate heat for 5 minutes before turning the chicken pieces and cooking for a further 5 minutes. Sprinkle with paprika.

Remove the chicken with a slotted spoon and arrange on top of the onion in the dish. Now return the frying pan to the heat and pour in the crème fraîche to deglaze the pan. Heat until just bubbling, while stirring and scraping the base and sides of the pan. Check and season with salt and pepper.

Pour the sauce over the chicken and cover the dish with foil. Transfer to the oven to cook for 15–20 minutes. Sprinkle with the chopped parsley and serve.

FREEZE
Put the onion in a freezer container and top with the pan-fried chicken and sauce. Cover with foil, cool quickly, seal and label, then store for up to 2 months.

TIP
Paprika powder can range from mild to hot, so make sure you use the mild variety for this recipe. You can use hot paprika, but add an additional carton of crème fraîche just before serving to balance the heat.

Quick Chicken Curry

This curry is full of flavour, hence the long list of ingredients – though more traditional versions have many more than this!

SERVES 4–6

3 tablespoons sunflower oil
4 large skinless chicken breasts,
   sliced into 2cm strips
Salt and freshly ground black pepper
2 large onions, finely chopped
1 tablespoon finely grated fresh
   ginger root
2 garlic cloves, crushed
½ red chilli, deseeded and
   finely chopped
½ teaspoon ground cardamom
¼ teaspoon ground cloves
1 tablespoon medium curry powder
1 tablespoon turmeric
1 teaspoon ground cumin
1 tablespoon plain flour
450ml Chicken Stock (see page 248)
2 tablespoons mango chutney
100ml full-fat plain yoghurt,
   or double cream

PREPARE AHEAD
The curry can be made without adding the yoghurt up to a day ahead. Reheat gently to serve and stir in the yoghurt.

Heat 2 tablespoons of oil in a deep frying pan. Season the chicken strips and brown quickly all over until sealed (you may need to do this in batches). Remove with a slotted spoon to a plate.

Add the onions and fry for a few minutes, then cover, lower the heat and fry for 10 minutes, until softened.

Remove the lid, increase the heat and add the ginger root, garlic and chilli and fry for 1 minute. Sprinkle in the ground spices and fry for a few minutes more. Sprinkle over the flour then stir in the stock and bring to the boil, until thickened.

Add the mango chutney and return the chicken to the pan. Season with salt and pepper. Lower the heat, cover and simmer for 5–10 minutes or until the chicken is tender. Add the yoghurt or cream and serve hot.

FREEZE
The curry freezes well but without the yoghurt.

AGA
First soften the onion in the simmering oven for 15 minutes. Add the chicken and return to the same oven for 10 minutes. Continue on the boiling plate.

Shiitake Mushroom Stir-fry

Stir-frying is one of the best ways of cooking vegetables: short and sharp, so the vegetables arrive on the plate still having plenty of texture, colour and food value. For everything to work smoothly and quickly, all the ingredients need to be prepared before you start to cook.

SERVES 6

3 tablespoons vegetable oil
2.5cm (1in) fresh ginger root,
    cut into very fine strips
2 garlic cloves, crushed
4 spring onions, diagonally sliced
1 small, trimmed head of celery, sliced
100g (4oz) mangetout, trimmed and
    sliced diagonally in three
1 red pepper, deseeded and
    cut into strips lengthways
150g (5oz) beansprouts
150g (5oz) shiitake mushrooms,
    thinly sliced
150g (5oz) white cabbage,
    very finely shredded
1 tablespoon dark soy sauce
1 tablespoon oyster sauce
Salt and freshly ground black pepper

Heat the oil in a large wok or frying pan until really hot. A simple method to test the heat of the oil is to put the point of a wooden chopstick in it. When the oil is hot enough it will immediately bubble around it.

Throw in the ginger and garlic and cook for about 10 seconds before adding the spring onions, celery, mangetout and red pepper. Cook for about 2 minutes, briskly turning the vegetables over and over in the oil. Add the beansprouts, mushrooms and cabbage. Cook for a further 2 minutes.

Add the soy and oyster sauces to the pan. Season with salt and pepper and serve immediately.

PREPARE AHEAD
Have all the vegetables prepared ready to fry: the garlic and ginger on one plate, spring onions, celery, mangetout and red pepper in a bowl. Put the beansprouts, mushrooms and cabbage in a separate bowl. Covered, the ingredients can be kept in the fridge for up to 6 hours before cooking.

AGA
Stir-fry on the boiling plate

Barnsley Chops with Onion Gravy

A Barnsley chop is a double chop, cut straight across the back of the lamb. These chops go well with Whipped Potatoes (see page 144).

SERVES 4
4 Barnsley chops
4 whole lambs' kidneys
Salt and freshly ground black pepper
4 teaspoons mint jelly

For the onion gravy
15g (½oz) butter
1 medium onion, grated
1 teaspoon plain flour
1 teaspoon Dijon mustard
3–4 tablespoons beer or dry white wine
1–2 teaspoons mint jelly
300ml (10fl oz) vegetable stock or
    Chicken Stock (see page 248)

PREPARE AHEAD
The boned, prepared chops enclosing the kidneys can be kept covered in the fridge for up to 24 hours.

AGA
Preheat a ridged grill pan on the boiling plate, brush the chops with a little oil, then put them in the grill pan and partially cover with a tilted lid. Cook for about 8 minutes, turning once. Then spread with the jelly.

Trim the excess fat from each chop, then carefully cut around and remove the central bone. Snip the central core from each kidney using a pair of scissors.

Curl the 'tails' of each chop around to enclose a kidney and use small skewers to hold the chop closed and keep the kidneys in position. Season with salt and pepper.

Preheat the grill to maximum for 5 minutes.

Position the chops in a foil-lined grill pan about 10cm (4in) away from the heat source. Grill for about 4 minutes, spread with half the mint jelly, then turn over and grill the other side for the same time. Spread with the remaining jelly and remove from the heat; cover and keep warm while you make the gravy.

Pour off any juices from the grill pan into a medium-sized frying pan. Melt the butter in the pan and stir in the onion. Cook over a moderate heat for 5 minutes until softened and slightly coloured. Add the flour, stir in the mustard, beer or wine and mint jelly and, when bubbling, pour in the stock.

Bring to the boil and boil briskly until reduced by about a third. Taste and season, adding a little more jelly, mustard or salt and pepper to balance the flavours.

Serve the chops with mash and with the gravy spooned around.

Really Posh Cottage Pie

This is a really special minced meat pie, which is made with Port and dried wild mushrooms – popular for all occasions.

SERVES 6

30g (1oz) dried wild mushrooms
2 tablespoons sunflower oil
1kg (2¼lb) lean minced beef
1 onion, chopped
2 garlic cloves, crushed
3 tablespoons plain flour
1 × 400g tin chopped tomatoes
150ml (5fl oz) Port
1 beef stock cube
Salt and freshly ground black pepper
2 tablespoons fresh thyme leaves, chopped
2 tablespoons Worcestershire sauce

For the potato topping
1kg (2¼lb) old, floury potatoes, peeled
Approx. 5 tablespoons milk
A large knob of butter
75g (3oz) mature Cheddar

PREPARE AHEAD
The pie can be made up to 8 hours ahead and kept in the fridge.

FREEZE
It freezes well without the potato topping. Defrost and spoon the mash on top, then cook as above.

AGA
The mince can be brought to the boil on the boiling plate, then covered and cooked in the roasting oven for an hour. Roast the completed dish on the second set of runners for 30 minutes until golden and bubbling.

Preheat the oven to 160°C/140°C fan/Gas 3. You will need a fairly shallow, 2.5-litre (4-pint) ovenproof dish.

Measure the dried mushrooms into a heatproof bowl and pour over 400ml (14fl oz) boiling water. Set aside to soak for 30 minutes then drain and reserve the liquid. Roughly chop the mushrooms.

Heat the oil in a frying pan, add the mince and fry until brown all over (you may need to do this in batches). Add the onion and garlic and fry for a few minutes.

Sprinkle over the flour, stir for a minute, then blend in the chopped tomatoes, Port and reserved mushroom liquid. Add the stock cube, stir and season with salt and pepper. Bring to the boil, cover and cook in the oven for 45 minutes – 1 hour, or until the mince is tender.

Remove from the oven and stir in the thyme and Worcestershire sauce then spoon into the dish and spread out evenly. Set aside to cool while you make the topping. Increase the oven temperature to 200°C/180°C fan/Gas 6.

Boil the potatoes in boiling salted water until tender, drain and return to the pan. Add the milk, butter, salt and pepper and mash until smooth.

Spread the potatoes over the cold mince and fork the top. Sprinkle with the cheese then place in the oven for 35–40 minutes, until bubbling and golden on top. Serve hot.

Garden Vegetable Cottage Pie

A good alternative for vegetarians to the usual cottage pie. For an informal buffet or supper, it is a good idea to serve one of each type of pie, side by side. Use the vegetables which are to hand or in season: onions, carrots, cauliflowers, leeks and celery would make a good wintery mix.

SERVES 6

2 tablespoons vegetable oil

25g (1oz) butter

1kg (2¼lb) mixed vegetables (see above)

50g (2oz) plain flour

1 × 400g tin chopped tomatoes

150ml (5fl oz) vegetable stock

300ml (10fl oz) milk

Salt and freshly ground black pepper

For the potato topping

1kg (2¼lb) old, floury potatoes, peeled

150ml (5fl oz) milk

1 × 125g tub full-fat fresh goat's cheese

25g (1oz) butter

PREPARE AHEAD
The pie can be made and kept covered in the fridge for up to 24 hours. Bake the pie in the top half of a preheated oven at 200°C/180°C fan/Gas 6 for 40 minutes or until bubbling hot and browned.

AGA
Cook on a top shelf in the roasting oven for about 20 minutes until golden brown.

You will need a flameproof dish about 30 × 20 × 6cm (12 × 8 × 2½ in). First, prepare the vegetables: cut larger vegetables such as carrots into dice, cauliflower into small florets, or leave tiny vegetables, such as baby sweetcorn, whole.

Heat the oil and butter together in a large pan, then stir in all the vegetables that take the longest to cook, such as carrots, onions and celery. Cook over a fairly high heat, stirring frequently, until the vegetables begin to brown a little. Sprinkle in the flour, stir and cook for 1–2 minutes. Pour in the chopped tomatoes, followed by the stock, then the milk. Bring to the boil, then cover and simmer over a low heat for 30 minutes.

Uncover and add the remaining vegetables (cauliflower, leeks, baby sweetcorn and so on) and continue to cook gently, stirring occasionally, for a further 20–30 minutes, or until all the vegetables are cooked. Taste and season carefully with salt and pepper. Cover and keep hot if aiming to serve soon.

Cook the potatoes in boiling salted water until soft. Leave to drain in a colander. Add the milk and goat's cheese to the pan and return to the heat. Season with salt and pepper and bring to the boil. Tip the potatoes back into the pan, remove from the heat and mash to a fluffy consistency with a potato masher or ricer.

Preheat the grill to high. Spread the vegetable mixture in the dish then gently spread the potato on top. Dot the top with butter and put under the grill for about 10 minutes or until browned and bubbling. Serve piping hot.

Pasta Amarilla

This is a creamy, smoky, pasta bake. There's no need to cook the fish before it is added to the rest of the ingredients, as it cooks beautifully when baked in the mixture.

SERVES 6–8

225g (8oz) penne pasta

1 onion, coarsely chopped

350g (12oz) undyed smoked haddock fillet, skinned and cut into 2.5cm (1in) thin strips

3 hard-boiled eggs, chopped

Juice of 1 lemon

Salt and freshly ground black pepper

For the béchamel sauce

900ml (1½ pints) milk

1 bay leaf

½ teaspoon black peppercorns

50g (2oz) butter

50g (2oz) plain flour

For the topping

150ml (5fl oz) double cream, seasoned

50g (2oz) Parmesan, grated

50g (2oz) Cheddar, grated

PREPARE AHEAD
Follow the recipe but don't add the cream topping. Cover and chill up to 24 hours ahead. Just before baking, pour over the cream and sprinkle with the cheeses. To reheat, bake in a preheated oven at 220°C/200°C fan/Gas 7 for about 35 minutes.

AGA
Cook on the second set of runners in the roasting oven for 20–25 minutes until golden brown and hot right through.

Preheat the oven to 220°C/200°C fan/Gas 7. Butter a 1.5 litre (3-pint) shallow ovenproof dish.

To make the sauce, pour the measured milk into a pan and add the bay leaf and peppercorns. Bring the milk to just below boiling point, then remove the pan from the heat, cover and leave aside to infuse for about 30 minutes.

Meanwhile, bring a large pan of salted water to the boil. Add the pasta and onion and cook according to the packet instructions. Drain.

To finish the béchamel sauce, melt the butter in a medium-sized pan, then pull the pan aside from the heat and stir in the flour. Gradually add the strained, infused milk, stirring quickly. Replace the pan over the heat and bring to the boil, still stirring, then allow to boil for about 2 minutes.

Add the strips of smoked haddock and stir well over the heat for 1 minute, then add the chopped hard-boiled eggs and lemon juice, followed by the drained pasta and onion. Mix well then taste and season carefully with salt and pepper.

Pour the mixture into the baking dish and level the top with the back of a spoon. Pour the cream over the top and sprinkle with the cheeses. Bake for 25 minutes or until golden brown and piping hot. Serve immediately.

FREEZE
Add an additional 150ml (5fl oz) milk to the béchamel sauce and omit the hard-boiled eggs. Turn into a freezer-proof baking dish without the topping and freeze for up to 1 month.

Spinach & Three Cheese Bake

A rather different style of pasta dish that makes a change from cannelloni or lasagne. You could use a 1.25kg bag of frozen leaf spinach, thawed and drained, if fresh is not available.

SERVES 4

300g (10oz) penne pasta

For the tomato sauce

1 tablespoon olive oil

1 onion, chopped

2 garlic cloves, crushed

25g (1oz) plain flour

300ml (10fl oz) vegetable stock or
    light Chicken Stock (see page 248)

1 × 400g tin chopped tomatoes

2 tablespoons tomato purée

2 teaspoons sugar

Salt and freshly ground black pepper

For the filling

225g (8oz) fresh young spinach,
    coarsely chopped (or see above)

2 tablespoons water

225g (8oz) full-fat mascarpone

50g (2oz) Parmesan, freshly grated

A small bunch fresh basil, chopped

2 teaspoons cornflour

50g (2oz) mature Cheddar, grated

PREPARE AHEAD

The dish can be fully prepared and kept covered in the fridge for up to 24 hours. Cook as above and serve.

AGA

Bake the completed dish on the second set of runners in the roasting oven for 25–30 minutes.

Preheat the oven to 220°C/200°C fan/Gas 7. You will need a shallow, 2-litre (4-pint) ovenproof dish.

Cook the pasta in boiling salted water according to the packet instructions until just cooked. Drain and refresh in cold water, then set aside.

Heat the oil in a frying pan and fry the onion for 5 minutes until it starts softening. Add the garlic and fry for a further minute.

Measure the flour into a bowl and mix with a little cold stock, stirring until smooth. Add the remaining stock and stir. Pour into the pan with the onion and garlic and bring to the boil, stirring.

Add the tinned tomatoes, tomato purée and sugar and season with salt and pepper. Bring to the boil, cover, lower the temperature and simmer for 10 minutes.

To make the spinach mixture, first fry the spinach in a pan for a couple of minutes with 2 tablespoons of water until just wilted. Drain and squeeze out any liquid, then set aside to cool.

Measure the mascarpone, Parmesan and basil into the pan, and return the spinach. Mix the cornflour with a little cold water and add to the pan. Bring to the boil, stirring, until the mascarpone has melted and the spinach is combined and the mixture has slightly thickened. Season with salt and pepper.

Stir the penne into the tomato sauce and spoon into the dish, season with salt and pepper. Spoon on blobs of spinach mixture randomly over the top. Sprinkle with the grated cheese. Bake for 25–30 minutes until golden brown and bubbling around the edges.

Garden Veg Curry

This is a simple, cheap curry to make and serve to friends, and you can easily double the quantities if you need to. Serve with shop-bought naan breads.

SERVES 6

900g (2lb) mixed vegetables,
    such as cauliflower, potatoes,
    turnip, carrots and leeks
4 tablespoons sunflower oil
2 large onions, chopped
2 fat garlic cloves, finely chopped
5cm (2in) fresh ginger root,
    peeled and finely chopped
½–¾ teaspoon chilli powder
1 × 400g tin chopped tomatoes
170ml (6fl oz) pineapple juice
150ml (5fl oz) vegetable stock
Salt

PREPARE AHEAD
The curry can be made, cooled, covered and kept in the fridge for up to 2 days. To reheat, place the curry in a large pan and heat gently until boiling and thoroughly warmed through.

Prepare the vegetables: cut the cauliflower into sprigs, cube the potatoes and turnip, dice the carrots and thickly slice the leeks.

Heat the oil in a large pan and add the chopped onions. Cook over a low heat for about 25 minutes, stirring occasionally, until the onion is nicely browned; do not allow it to burn.

Stir in the garlic and ginger and cook for a further 5 minutes. Stir in the chilli powder, tomatoes, pineapple juice and stock and bring to a simmer.

Add the vegetables. If you are using carrots, they take the longest to cook so they should go in first, 10 minutes ahead of the rest of the vegetables. Bring up to a gentle simmer, then cover and cook for 15 minutes.

Uncover and test the vegetables. They may need a further 5–10 minutes cooking until tender, depending on the size of the pieces. Taste and add salt if necessary. Serve hot with warm naan bread.

Peppers Stuffed with Spinach & Three Cheeses

A vegetable dish that is a meal in its own right, this is ideal for a family supper. Stuffed peppers are quite a classic dish – just serve with crusty bread.

SERVES 4–6

4 medium red or yellow peppers
1 tablespoon sunflower oil
Salt and freshly ground black pepper
1kg (2lb 4oz) fresh spinach or a 500g (1lb) pack frozen leaf spinach, thawed
75g (3oz) mature Cheddar, grated
75g (3oz) Gruyère or Emmental, grated
1 × 125g tub full-fat cream cheese
2 eggs, beaten

PREPARE AHEAD
The uncooked, stuffed peppers can be covered and kept in the fridge for up to 24 hours.

AGA
Cook on the grid shelf on the floor of the roasting oven for about 35–40 minutes, keeping covered for the first 20 minutes.

Preheat the oven to 190°C/170°C fan/Gas 5. You will need a roasting tin large enough to accommodate eight pepper halves.

Cut each pepper in half through the stem and down to the base. Use a small knife to cut away the central core and ribs but leave the stalk on. Arrange the peppers in the roasting tin, cut-side up, drizzle with a little oil and season with salt and pepper.

If using fresh spinach, wilt the leaves in a pan for a couple of minutes, refresh and drain. If using frozen spinach, thaw and drain. Use your hands to squeeze every last drop of water from the spinach, then put the leaves in a large mixing bowl with the remaining ingredients. Beat well to mix thoroughly, then taste and season with salt and pepper.

Spoon the mixture into the pepper halves, then cover the roasting tin with greased foil. Bake for 30 minutes. Remove the foil and bake for a further 15 minutes or until the peppers are tender when tested with the sharp point of a knife and the filling is puffed and browned. Serve hot.

Classic Duck with Crisp Sage & Onion

This recipe solves a very common cookery problem: how to roast duck until the skin is crisp without having the meat overcooked and dry. Here, there's a very traditional stuffing to serve with the bird. The ingredients are left fairly chunky and cooked separately from the duck, so the stuffing ends up very crisp and light. It is my mother's technique and to my mind, unbeatable. She often made it a day ahead.

SERVES 5–6

1 × 2.6kg (5½ –5¾lb) oven-ready duck

For the flavouring

1 large onion, cut into 6–8 wedges

1 lemon, cut into 6–8 wedges

1 generous sprig of fresh thyme

Salt and freshly ground black pepper

For the stuffing

450g (1lb) onions, very coarsely chopped

300ml (10fl oz) water

75g (3oz) butter

225g (8oz) soft white breadcrumbs

2 rounded teaspoon fresh chopped sage

Salt and freshly ground black pepper

Preheat the oven to 220°C/200°C fan/Gas 7. Grease a shallow baking dish about 25 × 20cm (10 × 8in) in which to bake the stuffing. You will also need a small roasting tin and a wire rack that will fit inside it on which to roast the duck.

To prepare the duck, remove any giblets and pull away the fat deposits from the interior at the rear end of the bird. These can be discarded or used for cooking if you wish.

Combine the flavouring ingredients in a bowl and toss together with a generous amount of salt and pepper. Put into the cavity of the bird, then use a skewer to close the body opening and prevent the ingredients falling out. Rub the duck skin with salt and pepper.

Place the duck breast-side down on the roasting rack in the tin. Roast in the top half of the oven for 30 minutes.

Make the stuffing. Put the onions and water together in a pan and bring to the boil. Cook for 10 minutes or until the onions are just tender but not soft. Drain and return the onions to the hot pan along with the butter. Once the butter has melted, stir in the remaining stuffing ingredients, seasoning generously with salt and pepper, and lightly toss together.

Spread the stuffing lightly in the prepared baking tin without pushing or compressing the mixture.

....

PREPARE AHEAD

The duck can be filled with the flavouring ingredients and stored in the fridge, uncovered, for up to 6 hours. (Keeping the duck uncovered helps the skin to stay dry so it will be crisper when roasted.) The stuffing can be made, put in the baking tin, covered and also stored in the fridge for up to 6 hours. Make sure the duck is removed 1 hour before roasting to allow it to come up to room temperature.

FREEZE

Don't freeze the duck. Put the cooked stuffing in a dish inside a plastic freezer bag, seal and label, then freeze for up to 1 month.

AGA

Roast the duck upside-down in the top section of the roasting oven for 30 minutes. Turn the right way up and roast for a further 25 minutes until golden, then transfer to the simmering oven for about 20 minutes until the legs are tender.

After the first 30 minutes, remove the duck from the oven, turn it over so it is breast-side up and baste it well. Transfer to the bottom half of the oven and put the stuffing in the top half. Continue to roast for a further 30 minutes.

At this stage, baste the duck again, then lower the oven temperature to 160°C/140°C fan/Gas 3. Continue to cook both the stuffing and the bird for a further 30 minutes or until the duck is thoroughly browned, crisp and cooked. The stuffing should be crisp and browned right through.

Serve the duck hot with generous spoonfuls of the stuffing. (The flavouring ingredients are not intended to be served.)

Stuffed Chicken Breasts with Roasted Potatoes & Onions

Stuffed chicken breasts with tasty liver, sausage meat and thyme stuffing, served with roasted potatoes and onions. This is an all-in-one dish, requiring only a green vegetable, such as green beans or broccoli.

SERVES 6

225g (8oz) pork sausage meat

175g (6oz) fresh chicken livers, roughly chopped

1 tablespoon fresh thyme leaves, chopped

3 tablespoons chopped parsley

Salt and freshly ground black pepper

6 boneless chicken breasts, skin on

900g (2lb) potatoes, peeled and diced into 2cm (¾in) cubes

2 large onions, roughly chopped

25g (1oz) butter, melted

2 tablespoons olive oil

PREPARE AHEAD
The chicken can be stuffed up to a day ahead and kept in the fridge until needed.

FREEZE
The chicken breasts can be frozen stuffed and uncooked.

Preheat the oven to 220°C/200° fan/Gas 7.

Measure the sausage meat, liver and herbs into a bowl, season with salt and pepper and mix with your hands to combine.

Arrange the chicken breasts on a board and loosen the skin, leaving one side attached. Season the chicken, then divide the stuffing into six and use to stuff under the skin of each breast. Pull the skin back over and smooth flat again.

Put the potatoes and onions in a large roasting tin, pour over the butter and oil, season with salt and pepper and toss together. Roast for about 25 minutes until lightly golden.

Arrange the chicken breasts around the roasting vegetables and return to the oven for about 30 minutes, until the chicken is cooked and golden and the vegetables and tender and crisp.

AGA
Roast the vegetables on the floor of the roasting oven for about 20 minutes. Add the chicken and roast for a further 30 minutes.

Chicken Pie with Chunky Potato Topping

This is a different kind of chicken pie, using cubed potato instead of mashed potato or pastry.

SERVES 6

300ml (10fl oz) white wine
600ml (1 pint) chicken stock
1 × 1.7kg (3½lb) whole chicken
2 bay leaves
5 sprigs of thyme
2 carrots, peeled and thinly sliced
2 leeks, halved and sliced
2 celery sticks, sliced
1kg (2.2lb) potatoes, peeled
   and sliced into 1cm cubes
75g (3oz) butter
75g (3oz) plain flour
Salt and freshly ground black pepper
100ml (3½fl oz) double cream
75g (3oz) mature Cheddar, grated

Preheat the oven to 180°C/160°C fan/Gas 4. You will need a deep saucepan that's wide enough to fit the whole chicken, and also a wide, 2-litre (4-pint) ovenproof dish.

Measure the wine and stock into the large saucepan and add the chicken, breast-side up. Add the bay leaves and thyme to the pan. Bring to the boil, cover and transfer to the oven for about 1 hour if your pan is ovenproof; you can also simmer the chicken in a covered pan over a gentle heat on the hob for an hour.

After an hour, add the carrots, leeks and celery, bring back to the boil, then return, covered, to the oven for a further 30 minutes or until the chicken is cooked and the vegetables are tender.

Remove the herbs and discard. Remove the chicken and vegetables from the pan and strain the cooking liquid into a jug so you have 900ml (1 ½ pints) – if you have a little less, add some more stock.

Remove the meat from the chicken carcass and slice into pieces. Tip into a bowl and add the reserved vegetables.

Put the cubed potatoes into a pan of cold salted water, bring to the boil and boil for 8–10 minutes or until just cooked. Drain.

PREPARE HEAD
The pie can be prepared up
to 12 hours ahead and then
cooked to serve.

FREEZE
The pie freezes well, once
prepared and ready for the
oven. Defrost thoroughly,
then bake as above.

AGA
Bring the chicken and
vegetables to the boil, cover
and transfer to the simmering
oven for 1¼ hours. Bake the
dish on the second set of
runners in the roasting
oven for 35 minutes.

Meanwhile, melt the butter in a saucepan over a high heat, add the flour and whisk for a minute. Gradually add the hot cooking liquid and whisk until you have a smooth, thick sauce. Season with salt and pepper.

Pour half the sauce over the chicken and vegetables in the bowl, mix together and spoon into the ovenproof dish. Set aside to cool.

Add the double cream to the remaining sauce. Add the cooked potatoes, season and pour over the chicken in the dish. Sprinkle with the cheese.

Increase the oven temperature to 200°C/180°C fan/Gas 6. Bake the dish for 35–40 minutes, or until lightly golden on top and bubbling around the edges. Serve hot.

Scrumpy Beef Casserole with Parsley & Horseradish Dumplings

Just a little bit different and packed with flavour. These dumplings were an experiment that worked well. I patted out the suet dough to a rectangle, spread it with a mixture of parsley and horseradish, then rolled it up like a Swiss roll, sliced it and put it on top of the stew: a sort of savoury, Chelsea bun-dumpling! All so simple and can be prepared well ahead.

SERVES 6–8

2 tablespoons olive oil

1kg (2¼lb) diced braising steak

1 onion, sliced

2 carrots, cut diagonally into
    5mm (¼in) slices

2 celery sticks, cut into 5mm
    (¼in) slices

25g (1oz) plain flour

500ml (16fl oz) strong dry cider

1 beef stock cube

A small bunch of fresh thyme

1 bay leaf

150g (5oz) button mushrooms, halved

1 tablespoon Worcestershire sauce

A dash of gravy browning

For the dumplings

175g (6oz) self-raising flour

75g (3oz) shredded suet

½ teaspoon salt

½ teaspoon freshly ground black pepper

Approx. 10 tablespoons cold water

3 tablespoons very hot horseradish

3 tablespoons chopped fresh parsley

Preheat the oven to 150°C/130°C fan/Gas 2.

Heat 1 tablespoon of oil in a large deep casserole dish. Brown the meat all over (you may need to do this in batches), then remove with a slotted spoon and set aside.

Heat the remaining oil in the pan, add the onion, carrot and celery and fry over a high heat for about 5 minutes.

Measure the flour into a small bowl, mix with a little cider and stir to make a smooth paste. Add the remaining cider and whisk until smooth. Pour into the pan, stir, then add the stock cube, thyme and bay leaf. Bring to the boil.

Add the beef to the pan, season with salt and pepper, cover and transfer to the oven for about 1 hour 45 minutes, or until the beef is tender. Add the mushrooms, Worcestershire sauce and gravy browning, and return to the oven for 15 minutes.

Meanwhile, prepare the dumplings. Mix together the flour, suet, salt and pepper in a bowl, then stir in enough water to bring them together in a soft but not sticky dough. Turn out on to a lightly floured work surface and pat or roll out to a 15 × 20cm (6 × 8in) rectangle.

PREPARE AHEAD
Prepare and cook the
casserole for 2 hours, then
cool quickly, cover and put
in the fridge. Prepare the
dumplings as far as forming
the dough into a roll, cover
closely with clingfilm and
put in the fridge. Both items
can be kept for up to 2 days.
Reheat the casserole over
direct heat, drop in the
dumplings then bake in the
oven following the recipe.

FREEZE
Prepare and cook the
casserole for 2 hours, then
cool quickly and place in a
freezer container for up to
6 months. Make the suet
dumplings, slice and freeze
for up to 6 months. Reheat
the stew and add the
dumplings, cooking in a
high heat until bubbling.

AGA
First cook in the simmering
oven for 2–3 hours or until
tender. Then bring to the
boil on the top, add the cider
and flour. and stir until the
mixture thickens. Top with
the dumplings and transfer to
the roasting oven fairly near
the top for about 25 minutes
or until crisp and done.

Stir together the horseradish and parsley
and a little salt and pepper to form a paste.
Spread this evenly over the surface of the
dough, right up to the edges. Roll up from
one short end, Swiss-roll style. Cover with
clingfilm and keep in the fridge until ready
to use.

After 2 hours, remove the casserole from
the oven and immediately increase the
temperature to 200°C/180°C fan/Gas 6.

Remove the suet roll from the fridge and
cut evenly into eight rounds. Arrange these
cut-side up on top of the meat, sitting in the
juices, seven around the outside and one in
the middle. Bring up to simmering point over
direct heat, then return to the oven to bake
for 30 minutes or until the dumplings start
to get a golden crust. Serve immediately.

Chicken & Sausage Bacon Bundles

Judy, who used to work with Lucy and me, gave us the idea for this recipe. It is a straightforward, brilliant idea that is ideal for family suppers or barbecues. Children love these with some good old tomato ketchup.

SERVES 4

8 skinless chicken thighs, boned
Salt and freshly ground black pepper
2 teaspoons finely chopped fresh sage
8 pork chipolata sausages
8 long rashers smoked streaky bacon, rind removed
A little vegetable oil, for brushing

Preheat the oven to 220°C/200°C fan/Gas 7.

Lie the chicken thighs flat, skinned-side down on the work surface. Season with salt and pepper and sprinkle with a little sage. Roll up a sausage in each thigh, then wind a bacon slice around the chicken.

Brush a roasting tin with oil, sprinkle with a little salt and pepper and put the meat into the tin. Brush each roll with oil, then bake for about 25 minutes or until browned and cooked.

PREPARE AHEAD
The prepared thighs can be kept covered in the fridge for up to 1 day.

FREEZE
The raw thighs can be frozen for up to 4 months. Defrost thoroughly before following the recipe above.

AGA
Cook in the roasting oven on the highest set of runners for about 25 minutes.

West Country Gratin

If you have overestimated the vegetables for Sunday lunch, here is the best way to use them up for a supper dish on Monday. Apart from the vegetables I have specified in the recipe, you could add leftovers such as peas, green beans, cauliflower or broccoli. And I have not listed any particular cut of bacon because it simply does not matter.

SERVES 6

450g (1lb) piece of bacon
450ml (16fl oz) dry cider
50g (2oz) butter
2 celery sticks, thinly sliced
225g (8oz) white of leek, thinly sliced
50g (2oz) plain flour
300ml (10fl oz) warm milk
225g (8oz) cooked carrots, sliced
225g (8oz) cooked, peeled potatoes,
    cubed
Salt and freshly ground black pepper
50g (2oz) mature Cheddar,
    coarsely grated
50g (2oz) Parmesan, coarsely grated

PREPARE AHEAD
The completed dish will keep
in the fridge for up to 1 day
ahead. Cook as above.

AGA
Bake in the roasting oven on
the grid shelf on the second
set of runners for about
20 minutes.

Choose a small pan with a well-fitting lid. Add the bacon and pour in the cider. Bring to the boil, lower to simmering point, then cover and cook gently for about 30 minutes or until cooked and really tender. Remove the bacon from the pan and leave to cool.

Return the pan to the heat and boil the cider juices, if not too salty, until reduced to 300ml (10fl oz). Leave on one side.

Heat the butter in a large pan and stir in the celery and leek and fry for a minute. Cover and cook gently for 10 minutes.

Sprinkle in the flour, stir and take the pan off the heat before gradually stirring in the milk, followed by the reduced cider. Bring to the boil, stirring. Simmer for 1–2 minutes then fold in the cooked vegetables and cook for a minute to heat through.

Preheat the grill to medium. Cut off the rind and excess fat from the bacon and cut the meat into sugar cube-sized pieces. Fold these into the sauce. Taste and season with salt and pepper.

Pour the mixture into a shallow, ovenproof dish and sprinkle with the cheeses. Place under the grill until golden brown and piping hot throughout.

Maple-spiced Chicken

So quick to do – chicken breasts with a sweet and sour flavour.

SERVES 4

4 boneless, skinless chicken breasts
1½ teaspoons Chinese five-spice powder
3 tablespoons maple syrup
3 tablespoons soy sauce
2 tablespoons olive oil
1 onion, thinly sliced
300ml (10fl oz) Chicken Stock
    (see page 248)
1 tablespoon cornflour

PREPARE AHEAD
The chicken can be marinated for up to 6 hours.

FREEZE
This freezes well marinated but uncooked.

AGA
Roast in the roasting oven for 20–25 minutes.

Put the chicken breasts in a wide bowl. Sprinkle in the five spice and coat over the breasts. Pour in the maple syrup and soy and mix again. Cover and transfer to the fridge to marinate for a minimum of 1 hour.

Preheat the oven to 220°C/200°C fan/Gas 7.

Remove the chicken from the marinade (reserve the marinade for the sauce) and sit the chicken in a small roasting tin. Drizzle over 1 tablespoon of oil. Roast for 20–25 minutes, or until golden brown and the chicken is cooked.

Heat the remaining oil in a pan. Add the onion and fry for 5 minutes, stirring until soft. Pour in the reserved marinade and stock and bring to the boil.

Measure the cornflour into a cup, mix with 2 tablespoons of cold water and pour into the sauce. Bring to the boil, stirring until thickened, season with salt and pepper.

Carve each chicken breast into three and serve with the hot sauce.

Pan-seared Salmon &
Vegetables with Thai Dressing

This dish can be prepared well ahead of time. If you are keen on oriental food, it could be that you have sesame oil and rice wine vinegar in the cupboard. By all means use 1 tablespoon of sesame oil to substitute for one of the tablespoons of olive oil in the dressing (no more, as the sesame oil has such a strong flavour), and rice vinegar can be used instead of white wine vinegar. But please do not rush out and buy these ingredients specially for this recipe; it simply is not worth it. Thai curry paste has a very hot flavour so if you are trying it for the first time, you might like to use just 1 teaspoon.

SERVES 6 AS A STARTER
OR 3 AS A MAIN COURSE
3 × 200g (7oz) salmon tail fillets,
   skin on
Olive oil

For the Thai dressing
6 tablespoons olive oil
3 tablespoons white wine vinegar
1 tablespoon caster sugar
2–4 teaspoons red Thai curry paste
Sea salt and freshly ground black pepper
3 red or yellow peppers
1 medium aubergine
2 tablespoons chopped fresh coriander

First, make the dressing by combining all the ingredients together in a screw-top jar. Screw the lid on firmly and shake well to mix. Leave the jar in the fridge to allow the flavours to develop while you prepare the remaining ingredients.

Cut the salmon tail fillets in half from the wide end towards the point of the tail. Brush the fish pieces all over with olive oil and season with sea salt and pepper.

Cut the peppers into strips about 5–10 mm (¼–½in) wide. Put into a bowl.

Similarly, cut the stem and base from the aubergine, then slice in half lengthways and into strips the same size as the peppers. Put into a separate bowl. Add 2 teaspoons of oil to each bowl, season well with salt and pepper, then mix with your hands to coat the vegetables completely.

To cook the salmon and vegetables, you can use either a cast-iron, ridged, stovetop grill pan, or a medium-weight, non-stick frying pan.

Preheat the pan over a moderate to high heat for 5 minutes. Sear the salmon slices for about 2 minutes on each side. To test if the fish is fully cooked throughout, make a small slit in the thickest part of the salmon. The flesh should be a matt pink throughout, not translucent. Remove the salmon pieces to a shallow serving dish, skin-side down, and drizzle a spoonful of dressing over each piece.

Return the pan to the heat for 2–3 minutes before adding the peppers. Continue to cook over a moderately high heat for about 4 minutes or until the strips are well coloured. Return them to the bowl and fry the aubergine strips in the same manner. When browned, add them to the bowl with the peppers.

Pour the remaining dressing over the vegetables and add the coriander. Gently mix and add more salt and pepper, if liked. Spoon into the serving dish alongside the salmon.

Sea Bass with Citrus Salsa

If sea bass are not available, two fat sardines or one trout per person could be substituted. This recipe also works really well on the barbecue.

S E R V E S 4

4 whole sea bass, about 350–375g
    (12–13oz) each, gutted and cleaned
8 sprigs of fresh tarragon
½ lemon, cut into slim wedges
A little olive oil
Sea salt and freshly ground black pepper
A little melted butter

For the citrus salsa
2 tablespoons olive oil
1 teaspoon white wine vinegar
2 small courgettes, quartered and
    thinly sliced
1 medium onion, finely chopped
Juice of 1 small lemon
Grated zest and juice of 1 lime
1 tablespoon chopped fresh parsley
1 tablespoon chopped fresh tarragon
2 tablespoons mango chutney

PREPARE AHEAD
Prepare the fish up to 6 hours ahead, put on a plate, wrap closely in clingfilm and keep in the fridge. The salsa can be kept covered in the fridge for up to 2 days, although the courgette will lose its bright green colour, so add more chopped parsley.

AGA
Preheat a roasting tin containing a little butter on the floor of the roasting oven for 5 minutes. When the butter has melted, add the fish then cook on the floor of the roasting oven for 7 minutes on each side. Or fry on a preheated, ridged grill pan on the boiling plate.

To make the salsa, put the oil and vinegar in a small pan and sauté the courgettes for about 2 minutes. Using a slotted spoon, remove to a bowl before adding the onion to the pan. Sauté again for about 2 minutes just until the onion loses its raw flavour, but retains its crispness.

Add the contents of the pan and the remaining ingredients to the bowl of courgettes and mix well. Cover, cool and leave in the fridge for about 4 hours to allow the flavours to develop.

Prepare the fish by trimming off the fins with a pair of scissors. Slash the fish with three gashes in the thickest part of the body. Strip the leaves from the tarragon into a bowl, add the lemon wedges, a drizzle of olive oil and some sea salt and pepper, then toss together using your hands. Pack the mixture into the belly of the fish then brush with melted butter and sprinkle with seasoning.

Preheat the grill to a moderate heat for about 5 minutes. Line the grill pan with foil, put in a grill rack and place the fish on top. Position the grill pan so the fish is about 10cm (4in) away from the heat source and grill for about 8 minutes on each side. To test if the fish is cooked, use the sharp point of a knife to pierce the thickest part of the fish; the flesh should be flaky and opaque.

To serve, remove the flavouring ingredients and serve the fish piping hot with the salsa.

Butterflied Lamb in Lemon Marinade

Butterflied lamb is a boned leg of lamb opened out flat, vaguely resembling the shape of a butterfly! (You can get the butcher to take the bone out of the leg, known as a butterfly cut.) The advantage of this cut is that being both thin and spread out it cooks quickly and there is lots of crispy meat for everyone. It can be roasted or barbecued. Serve this with a quick Minted Yoghurt Sauce (see page 249).

SERVES 6
2–2.5kg (4–5lb) leg of lamb
   (weight before boning)

For the marinade
Juice of 3 lemons
3 large garlic cloves, quartered
1 tablespoon mustard powder
1 tablespoon coarse grain mustard
4 tablespoons runny honey

PREPARE AHEAD
The meat can be left in the fridge, in the marinade, for up to 2 days.

FREEZING
This freezes well, marinated but uncooked.

You will need to start to prepare the dish a day ahead.

Mix together the marinade ingredients in a small bowl. Using two plastic bags large enough to contain the lamb, slip one inside the other. Put the lamb into the inner bag and pour in the marinade. Seal so no leakage can occur, then put in the fridge overnight (or as long as possible).

Remove from the marinade and transfer to a large roasting tin. Leave covered to allow the meat to come up to room temperature.

Preheat the oven to 220°C/200°C fan/Gas 7 and cook the lamb for about 15 minutes per 450g (1lb) boned weight. After 30 minutes, strain the marinade and pour over the lamb.

AGA
Put the meat in the large roasting tin and slide on to the lowest set of runners in the roasting oven. After 30 minutes, strain the marinade and pour over the lamb. Transfer the meat to the simmering oven for a further 40 minutes. Put back into the roasting oven for 5 minutes before serving, to crisp the skin.

Pappardelle with Tomato & Vodka Sauce

Rather an adult sauce! This recipe is the formula for relaxing everyone and getting a party going with a swing. If you can't get pappardelle, try making it with tagliatelle or fettucine instead.

SERVES 4–6

25g (1oz) butter
1 onion, chopped
2 garlic cloves, crushed
1 × 400g tin chopped tomatoes
100g (4oz) Parma, Black Forest
    or Serrano ham, chopped
150ml (5fl oz) vodka
1 × 200g carton full-fat crème fraîche
A small handful of fresh basil leaves
40g (1 ½ oz) Parmesan, grated
Salt and freshly ground black pepper
400–450g (14–16oz) pappardelle

To garnish
A good handful of small sprigs
    of fresh parsley
Parmesan, freshly grated

Melt the butter in a medium-sized, deep frying pan and fry the onion and garlic over a medium to high heat for about 5 minutes, until the onion is quite brown.

Pour in the tinned tomatoes and stir in the ham. Leave the mixture to simmer gently, uncovered, for about 10 minutes. Pour in the vodka and simmer, uncovered, for a further 5 minutes.

Add the crème fraîche and basil leaves and carry on simmering for 5–10 minutes, or until the mixture is a good consistency for coating pasta. Remove the sauce from the heat and add the Parmesan. Taste and season with salt and pepper if needed.

Meanwhile, cook the pasta in boiling salted water until al dente, then drain. Quickly toss the pasta with the sauce and sprinkle with parsley sprigs. Serve immediately with additional Parmesan.

TIP
A quick way to finely chop a large quantity of garlic – about 8 cloves – is to grate the peeled cloves on the coarse side of the grater.

FREEZE
You can freeze the sauce for up to 2 months.

PREPARE AHEAD
The sauce can be made ahead, quickly cooled, covered and kept in the fridge for up to 2 days. Bring to the boil in a pan before serving with the freshly boiled pasta.

AGA
Start in a non-stick frying pan on the boiling plate for a few minutes. Cover and transfer to the simmering oven for about 10–15 minutes or until tender. Then follow the recipe, cooking on simmering plate.

Pak Choi & Shiitake Stir-fry

Also known as bok choy, pak choi is a Chinese cabbage with broad, white, succulent stems and mildly mustard-flavoured green leaves. It looks something like Swiss chard and I cook it in a similar way, slicing off the leaves and cooking the stem end separately. In this recipe there is the option to cook the stems and add the sliced leaves 2 or 3 minutes before the end of cooking; or keep the leaves, cook them like spinach and serve with a later meal.

SERVES 4

2 tablespoons sesame or sunflower oil

1 small red pepper, deseeded and sliced

12 small spring onions, trimmed

2 sticks lemon grass, bulb section
   only, finely chopped

1 small fresh red chilli,
   deseeded and thinly sliced

2 fat garlic cloves, crushed

2.5cm (1in) fresh ginger root,
   peeled and cut into slivers

450g (1lb) pak choi, sliced, keeping
   white and green parts separate

175g (6oz) shiitake mushrooms, sliced

2 tablespoons oyster sauce

A dash of dark soy sauce

Heat the oil in a large wok or frying pan. When hot, add the pepper, spring onions, lemon grass, chilli, garlic and ginger and toss constantly over a high heat for about 1 minute.

Add the white pak choi and mushrooms and continue to fry, briskly tossing the vegetables for a further minute. Stir in the oyster sauce and pak choi leaves. Add a dash of soy sauce to season.

Toss and cook only for as long as it takes to get everything piping hot, then if cooked and seasoned to your taste, serve immediately.

PREPARE AHEAD
Have all the raw ingredients prepared and ready to cook; you can keep them chilled for up to 6 hours before cooking.

TIP
Be careful with the chilli. Handle it as little as possible and wash your hands thoroughly after preparing it, or wear rubber gloves if you prefer.

Chicken Breasts with Madeira & Tarragon Sauce

Serve this with mashed potato or swede and fresh spinach.

SERVES 6

40g (1½oz) butter
6 boneless, skinless chicken breasts
Salt and freshly ground black pepper
225g (8oz) small shallots,
    peeled and left whole
40g (1½oz) plain flour
120ml (4fl oz) Madeira
300ml (10fl oz) Chicken Stock
    (see page 248)
200g tub full-fat crème fraîche
A small bunch fresh tarragon,
    chopped

PREPARE AHEAD
The dish can be cooked ahead and reheated to serve; add the tarragon just before serving.

FREEZE
It freezes well cooked without the tarragon. Reheat and add the tarragon before serving.

AGA
Bring to the boil on the boiling plate, cover and transfer to the simmering oven for 20 minutes.

Preheat the oven to 200°C/180°C fan/Gas 6.

Melt the butter in a large frying pan. Season the chicken breasts and fry on both sides until golden brown; you may need to do this in batches. Set aside.

Add the shallots to the pan, fry over a high heat to brown. Remove with a slotted spoon on to the plate with the chicken and set aside.

Measure the flour into a small bowl and mix with the cold Madeira, stir until smooth.

Pour the chicken stock into the frying pan, add the Madeira and flour paste and bring to the boil, stirring until thickened. Return the chicken and shallots to the pan, stir, and season with salt and pepper.

Bring to the boil, cover with a lid and transfer to the oven for about 15–20 minutes or until the chicken is cooked. Transfer the chicken and shallots to a warmed serving dish.

Add the crème fraîche to the sauce and bring to the boil, stirring. Add the tarragon and check the seasoning. Pour over the chicken and serve hot with mash and spinach.

Marinated Seafood Kebabs

The difficulty with kebabs is to get everything to cook in the same amount of time. Choosing the right ingredients to cook together is the first step. The second is to cut them to the right size. Fish fillets have flesh that tapers away to nothing and so are not substantial enough to cook satisfactorily. It is much better to buy boned, skinned, thick fish steaks which can be cut into nice, large chunks of a similar size. This recipe also works well on the barbecue.

MAKES 12 SKEWERS
TO SERVE 6

450g (1lb) monkfish, boned and skinned
450g (1lb) salmon steaks, boned and skinned
8 baby courgettes, each cut into
   6 thick slices
12 raw tiger prawns, heads removed
Salt and freshly ground black pepper

For the marinade
4 garlic cloves, crushed
Grated zest and juice of 1 lime
2 tablespoons good olive oil

To serve
Citrus Salsa (see page 72) or
   Dill Pickle Sauce (see page 249)

PREPARE AHEAD
The fish can be left to marinate for up to 8 hours in the fridge.

Cut each fish into 24 even-sized chunks.

Combine the ingredients for the marinade in a large bowl, then gently turn the fish and prawns in the mixture. Cover and leave in the fridge for 1–1½ hours to marinate.

Thread two pieces of each kind of fish on to each of the 12 skewers, interspersing each piece with a slice of courgette and finishing with a slice of courgette and then a prawn. Season with salt and pepper.

Preheat the grill to very high for 5 minutes. Turn the heat down to between medium and high. Position the kebabs on a grill rack in a grill pan about 10cm (4in) away from the heat source and grill for about 10 minutes, turning once or twice.

Serve warm with your chosen sauce or salsa.

AGA
Arrange the skewers lengthways on the large grill rack in a large roasting tin. Slide on to the top set of runners of the roasting oven for about 5 minutes. Turn the kebabs over and return to the oven for a further 3–5 minutes until the fish is tender. Or cook on a preheated, ridged grill pan.

Monkfish & Prawn Curry

This slightly spicy, aromatic curry is full of flavour. Any firm white fish, such as monkfish, cod, sea bass fillet or halibut, works well. Increase the chillies if you like a hot curry.

SERVES 6

1 tablespoon olive oil

2 onions, chopped

1 red chilli, deseeded and finely chopped

1 tablespoon fresh ginger root, grated

1 ½ teaspoons ground cumin

1 ½ teaspoons ground coriander

1 tablespoon curry powder

½ teaspoon turmeric

½ teaspoon black mustard seeds

1 × 400g tin chopped tomatoes

300ml (½ pint) fish stock

1 teaspoon runny honey

Juice of ½ a lime

750g (1½lb) monkfish, cut into 5cm cubes

250g (9oz) peeled raw prawns

Salt and freshly ground black pepper

2 tablespoons chopped fresh coriander

PREPARE AHEAD
The sauce can be made up to 1 day ahead. Reheat the sauce before adding the fish and prawns.

FREEZE
The sauce freezes well. Reheat, as above, before adding the fish and the prawns.

Heat the oil in a frying pan. Add the onion and fry for about 5 minutes until it starts to soften. Add the chilli and ginger and fry for 1 minute. Sprinkle in the other spices and fry for one more minute.

Add the tomatoes, fish stock, honey and lime juice. Stir until combined and bring to the boil.

Add the cubed fish and prawns, lower the heat and gently simmer for about 5 minutes until the prawns are pink and the fish is cooked through – be careful not to overcook it, otherwise the fish will break up.

Season with salt and pepper, sprinkle over the coriander and serve.

AGA
The curry can be cooked on the simmering plate, as above.

Antipasti Pasta

A bit of a cheat! Fusilli pasta with all the wonderful added ingredients that you would have on a plate of antipasti. All the antipasti ingredients can be bought from a good deli counter in the supermarket.

SERVES 4–6

250g (9oz) fusilli or penne pasta

4 tablespoons olive oil

1 onion, finely chopped

1 red chilli, deseeded and
    finely chopped

2 garlic cloves, crushed

1 × 180g tub chargrilled pepper
    in oil, drained and sliced

1 × 175g tub artichoke hearts in oil,
    drained and quartered

150g (5oz) cherry tomatoes, halved

3 tablespoons chopped fresh basil

4 tablespoons fresh pesto

Salt and freshly ground black pepper

100g (4oz) Parmesan, coarsely grated

PREPARE AHEAD
The plain pasta can be cooked
up to 6 hours ahead. Toss in
to the vegetables to serve.
Not suitable for freezing.

AGA
Cook on the boiling plate.

Cook the pasta in boiling salted water as per the packet instructions. Reserve 100ml of the cooking water before draining.

Heat the oil in a frying pan and fry the onion for 5 minutes. Add the chilli and garlic and fry for a further minutes. Stir in the peppers, artichoke hearts, tomatoes, 2 tablespoons of chopped basil and the pesto. Add the reserved pasta water and season well, with salt and pepper.

Toss until piping hot, tip into a serving dish and scatter with the remaining basil and the Parmesan.

Seville Minted Chicken

An unusual but delightful flavour combination. If you have no chicken stock to hand, use a cube.

SERVES 6

12 chicken thighs, bone in and skin on
Salt and freshly ground black pepper
4 tablespoons extra thick-cut marmalade, preferably home-made, chopped
1½ tablespoons mint sauce from a jar
3 garlic cloves, crushed
Grated zest and juice of 1 orange

For the sauce
400ml (14fl oz) Chicken Stock (see page 248)
2 tablespoons cornflour
Salt and freshly ground black pepper

PREPARE AHEAD
Marinate up to 12 hours ahead and roast as in the recipe above. The sauce can also be made ahead and reheated.

FREEZE
Freeze cooked cold chicken for up to 3 months.

AGA
Cook the chicken at the top of the roasting oven for about 30 minutes.

Preheat the oven to 200°C/180°C fan/Gas 6. You will need a roasting tin large enough to hold the chicken thighs in a single layer.

Trim off any excess fat from the chicken thighs and slash the skin with a sharp knife. Sprinkle the base of the roasting tin with some salt and pepper and arrange the chicken on top.

Combine the marmalade, mint sauce, garlic and orange zest in a bowl and season with salt and pepper. Mix well and spread the mixture over the chicken. Roast for 35–45 minutes, basting once or twice with the pan juices until cooked.

Transfer to a warmed serving dish. Cover and keep warm while making the sauce.

Skim the surface fat from the pan juices by tilting the pan so the liquid flows to a corner. Use a tablespoon to take off the surface fat.

Pour a small amount of the measured stock into a bowl and mix with the cornflour. Pour the remaining stock and the orange juice into the roasting tin, combine together with the juices in the pan, then stir in the cornflour blend.

Bring to the boil, stirring briskly and scraping the base and sides of the tin. Simmer gently for 2–3 minutes then taste and season with salt and pepper if needed, perhaps adding a dash of sugar.

Pour the sauce over the chicken thighs and serve immediately.

Crisp Duck Breasts with Ginger Sauce

Crisp duck breasts that are tender and pink. The delicious ginger and soy sauce in this recipe is made using stem ginger, which is most often used in baking – the bulbs of ginger can be bought in jars of syrup from most supermarkets.

SERVES 6

6 duck breasts, skin removed
3 tablespoons stem ginger syrup
2 tablespoons soy sauce
A knob of butter
Salt and freshly ground black pepper

For the sauce
450ml (16fl oz) Chicken or
   Game Stock (see page 248)
1½ tablespoons cornflour
2 tablespoons dry Sherry
4 spring onions, sliced into
   needle slivers
2 pieces stem ginger, cut into
   thin matchsticks

PREPARE AHEAD
The duck breasts can be sealed ahead and chilled until needed. Roast for 10 minutes if cold. The sauce can be made up to a day ahead.

AGA
Roast the duck breasts on the top set of runners in the roasting oven for 8 minutes.

Preheat the oven to 220°C/200°C fan/Gas 7.

Put the duck breasts into a bowl. Pour over the ginger syrup and soy sauce, and mix so the duck breasts are coated. Leave to marinate in the fridge for about 1 hour.

Melt the butter in a hot fying pan. Remove the breasts from the marinade, season with salt and pepper and brown for 1 minute on each side until just sealed. Transfer to a baking sheet and roast for 8 minutes in the oven.

Measure the stock into a pan and bring to the boil. Mix the cornflour and Sherry together, stir until smooth, then add to the pan along with the marinade. Stir until boiling and thickened, add the spring onions and ginger, check the seasoning.

Rest the duck breasts for a good 5 minutes, diagonally carve each breast into three and serve with the sauce.

Aubergine Cannelloni-style

Great for vegetarians – a change from the usual nut roast! I prefer frozen chestnuts to the pre-packed version, but you could use either.

SERVES 6

3 large aubergines
4 tablespoons olive oil
600ml (1 pint) Passata Sauce
    (see page 248)
2 tablespoons sun-dried tomato paste
1 teaspoon brown sugar
50g (2oz) Parmesan, grated

For the chestnut filling
2 tablespoons olive oil
1 large onion, finely chopped
2 celery sticks, finely chopped
250g (9oz) frozen chestnuts,
    thawed and finely chopped
200g (7oz) chestnut mushrooms, chopped
Salt and freshly ground black pepper
1 teaspoon mixed spice
½ teaspoon allspice powder
½ teaspoon cinnamon
75g (3oz) fine, fresh wholemeal breadcrumbs
1 egg, beaten
25g (1oz) Parmesan, grated

PREPARE AHEAD
The dish can be prepared
up to 8 hours ahead and
cooked to serve.

AGA
Bake on the second set
of runners in the roasting
oven for 30 minutes.

Preheat the oven to 200°C/180°C fan/Gas 6. You will need a 2-litre (4 pint) wide-based ovenproof dish for this recipe.

To make the chestnut filling, heat the oil in a frying pan, add the onion and celery and fry over a high heat for 1 minute. Lower the heat, cover and cook for 10 minutes until soft.

Add the chestnuts and mushrooms and fry over a high heat for 5 minutes. Season with salt and pepper, sprinkle in the spices and breadcrumbs and stir in the egg and Parmesan. Spoon into a bowl and set aside to cool.

Slice each aubergine lengthways to give six slices about 1cm thick. Heat the oil in a frying pan and fry the aubergine slices for about 2 minutes on each side until golden brown and cooked. Season with salt and pepper and set aside to cool.

Measure the Passata Sauce, sun-dried tomato paste and sugar into a bowl, add salt and pepper, and stir until combined. Pour half into the dish.

Lay the aubergine slices on a board, divide the chestnut filling into 12 and spoon a pile on to the end of each slice. Roll up the slices to give cannelloni-shaped bundles. Arrange, seam-side down, on the tomato sauce in the dish. Pour over the remaining sauce and sprinkle over the Parmesan.

Bake for 30 minutes until golden and bubbling.

The Best Cod & Herb Fishcakes

Fishcakes are great to make with leftover mashed potatoes and they also freeze well.

MAKES 8

500g (1lb 2oz) cod fillet, skinned

500g (1lb 2oz) King Edward potatoes, peeled and cubed

6 tablespoons chopped fresh parsley

4 tablespoons chopped fresh chives

Finely grated zest of ½ lemon

3 tablespoons light mayonnaise

½ teaspoon Dijon mustard

Salt and freshly ground black pepper

1 egg, beaten

175g (6oz) fresh fine white breadcrumbs

A little butter and oil, for frying

PREPARE AHEAD
The fishcakes can be made up to a day ahead and kept in the fridge. Coat in egg and then breadcrumbs before frying, to serve.

FREEZE
The fishcakes will freeze well uncooked.

AGA
Fry the fishcakes on the boiling plate or on the floor of the roasting oven for 4 minutes on each side.

Preheat the oven to 200°C/180°C fan/Gas 6.

Butter a piece of foil and season with salt and pepper. Sit the cod on top and wrap in the foil to make a parcel. Place on a baking sheet and bake for 15 minutes until just cooked and opaque. Set aside to cool.

Boil the potatoes in salted water until tender, drain and return to the pan and mash until smooth. Tip into a bowl.

Break the fish into large pieces and add to the mash in the bowl. Add the herbs, lemon zest, mayonnaise and mustard and season with salt and pepper. Stir until mixed together.

Shape into eight fishcakes, about 2.5cm (1in) thick. Dip each fishcake into the beaten egg and coat in breadcrumbs. Chill for about 30 minutes.

Melt a little butter and oil in a frying pan, and fry the fishcakes for 4–5 minutes on each side until lightly golden and heated through. Serve hot.

Red Pepper, Mushroom & Leek Lasagne

This is full of flavour and perfect for vegetarians and meat-eaters alike.

SERVES 6–8
8 sheets of lasagne

For the tomato and vegetable sauce
2 tablespoons olive oil
2 leeks, chopped
2 Romano red peppers, diced
2 fat garlic cloves, crushed
40g (2½oz) plain flour
2 × 400g tins chopped tomatoes
1 tablespoon tomato purée
2 teaspoons caster sugar
500g (1lb 2oz) chestnut mushrooms, sliced
1 bunch of fresh basil, chopped
1 tablespoon balsamic vinegar
Salt and freshly ground black pepper

For the cheese sauce
100g (4oz) butter
75g (3oz) plain flour
900ml hot milk
1 tablespoon wholegrain mustard
300g (10oz) mature Cheddar, grated

PREPARE AHEAD
The lasagne can be made completely up to 24 hours ahead.

AGA
Bake on the second set of runners in the roasting oven for 35 minutes.

Preheat the oven to 220°C/200°C fan/Gas 7. You will need a 3-litre (5-pint), ovenproof dish.

To make the tomato and vegetable sauce, heat the oil in a frying pan. Add the leeks and fry for 3 minutes, then add the peppers and fry for 5 minutes until the vegetables are soft. Add the garlic and season with salt and pepper.

Measure the flour into a bowl. Mix with half a tin of chopped tomatoes and stir until smooth. Add the remaining tomatoes to the vegetables in the pan, followed by the purée and sugar and then the flour mixture.

Bring to the boil, stirring until thickened, then add the mushrooms and boil for a couple of minutes, stirring. Add the basil and vinegar and check the seasoning.

To make the cheese sauce, melt the butter in a saucepan, add the flour and whisk over the heat for a minute. Gradually blend in the milk and whisk until bubbling and smooth. Add the mustard, three-quarters of the cheese and season with salt and pepper.

Spoon a third of the vegetable sauce into the base of the dish. Spoon over a third of the cheese sauce and sprinkle with a third of the remaining cheese. Lay three sheets of lasagne on top (break the lasagne so they fit neatly without overlapping). Continue with the remaining layers to give 2 layers of pasta and three layers of sauce and finish with the remaining cheese on top.

Bake in the preheated oven for 40 minutes until bubbling and golden brown.

Quite the Best Fish Bake

Full of flavour with a quick white sauce, and a hint of lemon and cheese. Just serve with petit pois or home-grown beans. A great change from the classic fish pie.

SERVES 6

650g (1lb 4oz) undyed smoked
    haddock fillet, skinned
650g (1lb 4oz) potatoes, peeled
225g (8oz) baby spinach, washed
6 hard-boiled eggs, peeled
    and quartered

For the sauce
300ml (½ pint) milk
50g (2oz) butter
50g (2oz) flour
200ml tub full-fat crème fraîche
Salt and freshly ground black pepper
75g (3oz) mature Cheddar,
    coarsely grated
Juice of ½ a lemon

PREPARE AHEAD
It can be made up to 8 hours ahead and kept in the fridge.

AGA
Cook the dish on the second set of runners in the roasting oven for about 25 minutes.

Preheat the oven 200°C/180° C fan/Gas 6. You will need a shallow ovenproof dish about 15 × 20cm (6in × 8in).

Measure the milk for the sauce into a saucepan and add the haddock. Bring to simmering point for 3 minutes. Lift out the fish and flake into pieces. Set aside and reserve the hot milk.

Cut the peeled potatoes into small chunks (about the size of a walnut) then boil in salted water for 10 minutes or until just cooked. Drain and refresh in cold water, drain again.

Heat a large frying pan over a high heat and cook the spinach until just wilted, drain in a colander and press with the back of a spoon to release any liquid.

To make the sauce, melt the butter in a saucepan, whisk in the flour and cook for 1 minute. Whisk in the reserved milk and crème fraîche and bring to the boil, stirring until thickened. Season with salt and pepper. Stir in half the cheese followed by the lemon juice and cooked potatoes. Stir well.

Arrange six piles of spinach in the base of the dish, top with haddock flakes and pieces of egg. Season with salt and pepper. Pour over the potatoes and sauce and sprinkle with remaining cheese.

Bake for 25 minutes until golden on top and bubbling at the edges. Serve hot.

Lamb Paysanne & Spinach Stuffing

Lamb cooked this way is wonderfully moist and does not need basting during cooking. The bonus is that the meat and vegetables are all ready at the same time. Incidentally, I do find a meat thermometer very useful, as you will see from this recipe.

SERVES 8

1.5–2kg (3½ –4½lb) boned shoulder
    or leg of lamb
2 large, mild onions, each cut into
    8 wedges
8 whole garlic cloves, skin on
2 medium aubergines, thickly sliced
1 yellow pepper, deseeded and
    cut into 8 sections
2 red peppers, deseeded and each
    cut into 8 sections
Salt and freshly ground black pepper
A sprig of fresh rosemary or
    a little dried rosemary

For the spinach stuffing
450g (1lb) fresh spinach leaves, shredded
1 garlic clove, crushed
125g (4½oz) full-fat cream cheese
25g (1oz) fresh white breadcrumbs
Salt and freshly ground black pepper

PREPARE AHEAD
The shoulder can be stuffed
up to 24 hours ahead and
stored in the fridge.

FREEZE
Freezes well stuffed and
uncooked.

Preheat the oven to 220°C/200°C fan/Gas 7. Grease a large roasting tin with oil. Begin by preparing the stuffing. Put the spinach and garlic into a large frying pan. Stir-fry over a high heat until the leaves have wilted and no excess liquid remains. Drain and cool.

Squeeze any remaining liquid from the spinach and transfer the leaves to a bowl. Beat in the remaining stuffing ingredients then taste and season with salt and pepper.

Trim off the excess fat from the lamb then stuff where the bone was with the spinach mixture. Put the joint in the middle of the roasting tin, surrounded by the onions and garlic, and roast for 25 minutes until the meat has browned.

Add the rest of the vegetables to the tin and turn the meat over. Season well with salt and pepper and sprinkle the lamb with a little rosemary. If using a meat thermometer, put it into the thickest part of the joint, then return the tin to the oven for about 1 hour until the lamb is cooked to your taste: the thermometer should read about 80°C for well done, 70–75°C for medium.

Carve and serve the meat with the vegetables and any pan juices. You can, if you like, eat the garlic; if you press one end of the clove it will come out like toothpaste at the other and taste mellow and delicious.

AGA
Slide the roasting tin on to the lowest set of runners in the roasting oven for 25 minutes. Return all the vegetables and meat to the same position in the oven and roast for about 1 hour until done.

Chicken with Vermouth & Sage

This recipe serves four, but can be readily expanded to serve six or eight. Very quick, it's a supper dish that can be on the table in a twinkling. Use Parma, Serrano or Black Forest ham, whichever is the best buy. Note the sauce is fairly thin as it contains no flour or butter.

SERVES 4

4 boneless, skinless chicken breasts
2 tablespoons chopped fresh sage
Salt and freshly ground black pepper
8 slices prosciutto or other dry cured ham
1 tablespoon olive oil
15g (½oz) butter
150ml (4fl oz) dry vermouth
1 × 200g tub full-fat crème fraîche

PREPARE AHEAD
This dish is so quick it is hardly worth preparing ahead. However, the rolled up chicken strips can be kept covered in the fridge, ready to cook, for up to 8 hours.

AGA
Cook on the boiling plate.

Slice each chicken breast in half lengthways. Scatter with 1 tablespoon of chopped sage then season with a little black pepper. Roll up each strip in a slice of prosciutto.

Heat the oil and butter in a large frying pan. Place the chicken rolls in the pan, seam-side down to prevent them unrolling, then cover and cook over a moderate heat for 2–3 minutes. Turn the rolls and cook for a further 2–3 minutes or until nicely browned.

Spoon off the fat from the pan, then pour in the vermouth. Cover and cook gently for a further 5 minutes. Transfer the chicken to a warmed serving dish; cover and keep warm.

Add the crème fraîche and remaining chopped sage to the pan. Bring to the boil and reduce slightly, stirring and scraping the base and sides of the pan. Taste and season with salt and pepper if necessary, then pour the sauce over the chicken. Serve hot.

Pheasant Casserole with Thyme & Prunes

The ideal winter recipe and a good way to cook older pheasants or perhaps pheasants that have been in the freezer for longer than you can remember!

SERVES 6

2 whole oven-ready pheasants
250g (9oz) smoked bacon lardons
2 onions, sliced
2 celery sticks, sliced
2 carrots, sliced
200ml (7fl oz) red wine
6 large pitted dried prunes, chopped
25g (1oz) plain flour
200ml (7fl oz) cold game or chicken stock
6 sprigs of thyme
1 tablespoon redcurrant jelly
Salt and freshly ground black pepper

PREPARE AHEAD
The casserole can be made up to a day ahead. Reheat the sauce with the breasts and legs and serve hot.

AGA
Bring to the boil, cover and transfer to the simmering oven for 2 hours.

Preheat the oven to 180°C/160°C fan/Gas 4.

Heat a large, deep frying casserole and brown the pheasants on all sides until lightly golden all over. Remove from the pan and set aside.

Add the bacon to the pan and fry over a high heat until crisp. Add the vegetables, fry for a few minutes, then add the red wine and prunes, and boil for a couple of minutes.

Measure the flour into a bowl and mix with the cold stock until smooth and pour into the pan. Bring to the boil, stirring, until thickened.

Add the thyme, redcurrant jelly, some salt and pepper and then the pheasants. Cover and transfer to the oven for about 1½ hours. Check if the breasts are cooked, if so carve from the carcass and return the carcass and legs to the pan and continue to cook for a further 30 minutes or until tender.

Remove the legs and serve hot with the breasts and the vegetables and sauce. If preferred, all the meat can be taken off the bone in manageable pieces and served with the sauce and vegetables as a casserole.

Fast-roasted Lamb with Lemon & Thyme

The lamb fillet I use for this recipe is the eye of the best end of neck chops. It is not suitable to use scrag end neck of lamb fillet as this would toughen with this very hot, short method of cooking. The sauce is simple and just enough for the four servings. English lamb is at its best and cheapest in early autumn.

SERVES 4

50g (2oz) butter, softened

2 tablespoons mint or redcurrant jelly

3 fat garlic cloves, crushed

1 tablespoon chopped fresh thyme leaves

2 loin fillets of lamb

Grated zest and juice of 2 lemons

1 tablespoon of redcurrant jelly

1 teaspoon cornflour

To garnish

A sprig of fresh thyme

PREPARE AHEAD

The meat can be marinated then browned up to 6 hours ahead, before roasting to serve.

AGA

Heat the grill pan on the boiling plate. Cook the fillets for 1 minute on each side until well browned. Put the meat in the small roasting tin, spread with the flavoured butter, then transfer to the top of the roasting oven and cook for 8–10 minutes.

Start this recipe at least one day ahead.

Combine the butter, mint or redcurrant jelly, garlic and thyme and spread over the meat surface. Cover and keep in the fridge for up to 2 days to allow the flavours to develop and permeate the meat.

Bring the lamb up to room temperature. Scrape off the flavoured butter and keep. When the meat's ready, preheat the oven to 220°C/200°C fan/Gas 7.

Heat a non-stick pan over a moderate heat for 1 minute. Place the lamb fillets in the pan and cook for 1 minute on each side or until dark brown.

Transfer to a small roasting tin and roast in the oven for 8–10 minutes, then remove from the oven and cover the tin with foil. Leave aside in a warm place to allow the meat to rest and 'set'.

Make up the juices in the pan to 250ml (8fl oz) with water (measure the juices in a measuring jug then add water) then add the lemon juice and redcurrant jelly and bring to the boil. Blend 2 tablespoons of water with the cornflour and add to the pan. Bring to the boil again, stirring continuously.

Carve each fillet fairly thinly on a slight diagonal. Spoon the pan juices over the meat and serve at once, garnished with a sprig of fresh thyme.

Pheasant Normandy-style

This is an excellent way to cook pheasant legs, which can be tough if not slow-cooked until tender. Also try the recipe with chicken joints; they'll take less time in the oven.

SERVES 6–8

25g (1oz) butter

1 tablespoon oil

8 pheasant leg joints or a brace
    of pheasant, jointed

40g (1½oz) plain flour

450 ml (15fl oz) dry cider or dry white wine

2 onions, cut into thin wedges

4 small dessert apples, peeled, cored
    and cut into eight

1 teaspoon fresh rosemary leaves, chopped

1 rounded tablespoon apple or
    redcurrant jelly

5cm (2in) cinnamon stick

Salt and freshly ground black pepper

150ml (5fl oz) full-fat crème fraîche

PREPARE AHEAD

The pheasant can be prepared to the point where it is removed from the oven, quickly cooled, then covered and stored in the fridge for up to 2 days. Reheat in a preheated oven at 160°C/140°C fan/Gas 3 for 20–30 minutes or over a low heat on top of the stove, then stir in the crème fraîche.

FREEZE

Do not add the crème fraîche and then the cooked, cold pheasant can be frozen for up to 2 months. Defrost thoroughly before adding the crème fraiche.

Preheat the oven to 160°C/140°C fan/Gas 3. You will need a flameproof casserole large enough to hold the pheasant joints comfortably in a single layer.

Heat the butter and oil in a large, non-stick frying pan and fry the pheasant joints until evenly browned all over, then remove to a casserole.

Pour off all but about 2 tablespoons of fat from the pan. Add the flour, then stir in the cider or wine and allow to thicken over the heat for a few minutes. Add the onions, apples, rosemary, apple or redcurrant jelly and cinnamon and season with salt and pepper. Bring to the boil, then pour over the joints in the casserole. Cover and transfer to the oven to cook for at least 1½ hours or until tender.

Use a slotted spoon to remove the joints to a serving dish, cover and keep warm.

Boil the remaining sauce, reducing if necessary to a thick sauce consistency. Stir in the crème fraîche. Retrieve and discard the cinnamon, then taste and season with salt and pepper. Bring to simmering point once more, then pour the sauce over the pheasant.

AGA

Once the cider or wine has been added and the pheasant joints replaced in the casserole, bring the mixture to a gentle boil, then cover and transfer to the simmering oven for about 1½ hours or longer, until tender.

TIP

Hen pheasants make the best buy. They are usually smaller, but more plump and tender than the male bird. If you have no idea of the age of a pheasant, don't risk roasting it, always use it for a casserole.

Red Pepper & Fennel Pissaladière

....

Or, in other words, fennel, peppers and onions on a deliciously crisp cheese-pastry base.

SERVES 8

For the pastry
175g (6oz) plain flour
75g (3oz) chilled butter, cut into cubes
75g (3oz) mature Cheddar, grated
1 heaped teaspoon English
    mustard powder
A good pinch of cayenne
1–2 tablespoons cold water

For the topping
6 large red peppers
1 tablespoon olive oil
2 Spanish onions, thinly sliced into rings
2 small fennel bulbs, sliced lengthways
2 garlic cloves, crushed
2 tablespoons chopped fresh parsley
1 teaspoon balsamic vinegar
Salt and freshly ground black pepper

To garnish
A few shavings of fresh Parmesan
Approx. 6 fresh basil leaves,
    torn in pieces

You will need a large, flat baking tray.

To make the pastry, put the flour and butter in a food processor and process until the mixture resembles breadcrumbs. Alternatively, put the ingredients in a large bowl and rub together with your fingertips.

Add the remaining ingredients and process, or mix together just enough for the pastry to form a ball. Wrap the pastry in cling film and put in the fridge while making the topping.

Preheat the grill and line the grill pan with foil.

Arrange the peppers in the foil-lined grill pan and grill, turning regularly, until blackened all over. Remove the peppers to a shallow dish, stacking them on top of each other, then cover with a plate and leave to cool. When ready, grasp the green stalk of each pepper and give it a twist to remove the central core and seeds. Strip off all the skin, then halve the peppers over the dish to catch the juices, then cut each one into six strips.

Heat the olive oil in a large frying pan, then stir in the onions and fennel. Fry until beginning to soften and colour, then cover and cook gently for about 30 minutes or until tender. Add the garlic and any pepper juices, then turn up the heat and cook until the excess liquid has evaporated. Add the peppers, parsley and vinegar, then taste and season with salt and pepper. Re-cover and leave aside until cold.

PREPARE AHEAD
The filling can be prepared, closely covered with clingfilm and kept in the fridge with the rolled-out pastry on the baking tray.

FREEZE
The dish is best not frozen, although if some is left over, freeze the remaining wedges for up to 2 weeks.

AGA
The onion and fennel can be cooked in a pan on the floor of the simmering oven for 30–35 minutes. Bake the pissaladière on the floor of the roasting oven for 20 minutes.

Put the dough in the centre of the baking tray and roll out to a 30cm (12in) circle. Pinch the edge between thumb and forefinger to create a rim. Return the tray to the fridge for 30 minutes.

Preheat the oven to 200°C/180°C fan/Gas 6.

About 20 minutes before serving, spread the vegetable mixture over the pastry up to the raised edge. Bake for 20 minutes or until the edge of the pastry is golden. Top with shavings of Parmesan and torn basil leaves and serve.

Avocado Tuna Pasta Salad

Cold pasta dishes have never been a favourite of mine, but this recipe is an exception. It is a combination of tuna, hard-boiled eggs and avocado mixed with a comparatively small amount of cooked pasta shells, and the ratio seems exactly right. It is simplicity itself to make and it looks good on a buffet table if you follow the instructions for the garnish.

SERVES 6–8
150g (5oz) pasta shells or penne pasta
3 × 185g tins tuna in oil
150ml (5fl oz) light mayonnaise
Salt and freshly ground black pepper
3 hard-boiled eggs
1 just ripe avocado
Juice of 1 lemon
3 tablespoons snipped fresh chives

To garnish
Long chives
About 6 black olives in oil, pitted
and halved

PREPARE AHEAD
The prepared salad, without the avocado, will keep covered with clingfilm for up to 24 hours. Add the avocado just before serving.

Cook the pasta shells in boiling salted water according to the packet instructions, until al dente. Drain in a colander, then rinse under cold running water to cool quickly. Tip the well-drained pasta into a large bowl.

Empty the tins of tuna into a sieve set over a bowl and leave to drain. Flake the tuna into the bowl that contains the pasta. Do not discard the drained juices.

Measure the mayonnaise in a jug, then stir in 2 tablespoons of the tuna juices. Season with salt and pepper.

Peel and chop the cold, hard-boiled eggs into largish pieces and add to the pasta and tuna, followed by the mayonnaise. Turn the mixture gently to mix. Taste and season with salt and pepper, then cover the bowl with clingfilm and chill until ready to serve.

Just before serving, peel and dice the avocado and toss in lemon juice. Add the avocado, lemon juice and chives to the salad, toss lightly together, then taste and add more seasoning if necessary.

Serve the salad in a large, shallow serving dish. Create a diamond pattern on its surface with the long chives and put a halved olive in the centre of each diamond. Serve lightly chilled.

Chilled Celebration Salmon

A magnificent cold salmon makes a marvellous centrepiece for a cold buffet. But even an enthusiastic cook is unlikely to have a metre-long poaching pan in which to cook the fish. Home cooks are far more likely to have a preserving pan or large stock pot, so here is a recipe, blissfully simple, that uses a round pan to give the salmon a semi-circular curl. The method guarantees perfectly cooked salmon and a four-star presentation. Serve with Fresh Herb Sauce (see page 249).

SERVES 10–12

2kg (4½lb) whole salmon, gutted

For poaching the salmon
Approx. 7 litres (12 pints) water
1 tablespoon salt
1 tablespoon peppercorns
2 bay leaves
Pared zest of ½ a lemon
½ a lemon, cut into wedges

To garnish
1 small cucumber, thinly sliced
20 whole, cooked prawns,
    peeled, with the heads on
A generous bunch of fresh dill
12 wedges of lemon

You will need a large stock pot or preserving pan that is about 30cm in diameter and with 22 litres capacity. You may also find a pair of rubber gloves useful.

Fold a strip of foil to make a 2.5cm wide band. Put this into the pan in a north–south direction, following the shape of the pan down the side, across the base and up the other side. Now put in a second, similarly folded, foil strip, in the same way as the first, but in an east–west direction.

Put all the poaching ingredients into the pan, cover and bring to a full boil.

For the next stage you might find it helpful to wear rubber gloves to protect your hands from the hot water. Turn the salmon belly-side up and hold on to the head with one hand and the tail with the other. Bring the salmon round into a gentle curl and hold that position while you put the fish into the pan, still belly-side up, so it curls around the shape of the pan.

Bring the water back to a full, rolling boil over a high heat, then boil gently for 2 minutes. Remove the pan from the heat. Cover with a lid and leave aside for about 2½ hours, or until the salmon has cooled just sufficiently to handle. I have found that the hotter it is, the easier it is to peel off the skin.

Again, you might find it helpful to wear rubber gloves to retrieve the salmon from the poaching water with the aid of the foil strips. Place the salmon straight on to a serving tray or plate so it is upright, in the position it is to be served.

Working fairly quickly, skin the salmon from head to tail while it is still hot, removing fins from the side and central back. Trim the tail fin into a neat shape with scissors. The skinned salmon should be a uniform, unblemished colour. Clean the serving plate carefully before starting to garnish the fish.

Arrange a line of halved cucumber slices down the backbone of the fish and around the base of the salmon, on the plate. Interlink the tails of the prawns and arrange 1 pair on the head of the salmon and 1 pair on the tail. Use sprigs of dill laid in the same direction to cover the base of the serving dish, and sprigs to garnish the head, centre back and tail. Now use the remaining prawns, cucumber slices and lemon wedges to garnish the plate and make it look as fresh and attractive as possible.

Serve the salmon lightly chilled soon after garnishing. Each person should be given a serving of fish, 2 prawns, a lemon wedge and some cucumber accompanied by the herb sauce.

Mosaic of Salmon en Croûte

To be honest, this recipe takes a little time and effort but the result is wonderful in both appearance and taste. It consists of a long roll of puff pastry that contains a dill-flavoured salmon mousse studded with nuggets of salmon wrapped in spinach – but this description hardly does it justice. It can be served hot, or cold with Fresh Herb Sauce (see page 249) and a dressed green salad.

SERVES 10

2 × 750g (1½lb) pieces of salmon
    fillet, skinned
500g (1lb 2oz) fresh spinach leaves
300g (10oz) salmon fillet, skinned
1 egg white
1 bunch of fresh dill, chopped
Salt and freshly ground black pepper
350g (12oz) puff pastry
1 egg, beaten

Preheat the oven to 220°C/200°C fan/Gas 7. Line a baking sheet with baking parchment.

Place the two large pieces of salmon fillet on to a board. Slice each one in half lengthways to give four long strips.

Cook the spinach with 3 tablespoons of water in a large frying pan until just wilted (you may need to do this in batches). Tip into a colander, refresh in cold water and drain well and squeeze out any excess water.

Slice the second quantity of salmon fillet into small pieces and put into a processor. Add the egg white, dill and salt and pepper and whizz until chopped. Add the cooked spinach and whizz until a smooth paste. Transfer to a plate.

Roll out the pastry to a large rectangle longer and wider than the four large pieces of salmon. Transfer to the baking sheet. Spread a third of the spinach paste over the centre of the pastry the same length and width as the salmon. Put two strips of fish on top, leaving a 2cm gap in between.

Use another third of the spinach mixture to fill the gap between the salmon fillets and to spread over the top of the fillets. Place the remaining strips of fish on top of the paste, mirroring the salmon underneath. Use the remaining third to fill in the gap and spread over the top.

Brush the pastry around the fish with beaten egg and fold in the ends then fold up the sides and seal on top. Carefully turn over so the seal is underneath. Cover and chill for 1 hour to firm up.

Glaze with beaten egg, score the top of the pastry and bake for 35–40 minutes, until golden brown and the pastry is crisp. If serving the pie hot, allow it about 10 minutes to settle. I think it is best served warm because it holds its shape well.

Cool Minted Chicken

We all know and love Coronation Chicken. This is a little lighter and fresher in flavour, is very easy to prepare, and is improved if it is made the day before without curry spices. Serve with hot garlic bread and salad.

SERVES 6

350g (12oz) freshly cooked chicken meat
150ml (5fl oz) half-fat crème fraîche
150ml (5fl oz) light mayonnaise
2 tablespoons chopped fresh mint
1 spring onion, finely chopped
Juice of ½ a lemon
¼ teaspoon sugar
Salt and freshly ground black pepper

To garnish
Sprigs of fresh mint

Cut the chicken into bite-sized pieces, removing all the skin and any small gristly pieces.

Mix together the remaining ingredients except the salt and pepper, fold in the chicken pieces, then taste and season carefully. Cover and chill in the fridge for 12 hours or overnight.

When ready to serve, taste and check the seasoning once more, then spoon out on to a dish and decorate with fresh mint.

Onion & Cheese Tart

The carton of soured cream is divided between the pastry and filling. It is an unusual ingredient in pastry but it makes one that handles well and tastes wonderful. You may prefer to cook the onions in the oil drained from the jar of olives – the extra olive flavour is too good to lose.

SERVES 8

For the pastry
225g (8oz) plain flour
175g (6oz) butter, cubed
1 tablespoon fresh thyme leaves
Freshly ground black pepper
1 × 300ml carton soured cream

For the filling
3 tablespoons olive oil
4 large, mild Spanish onions, sliced
1 teaspoon brown sugar
2 teaspoons balsamic vinegar
4 eggs
3 tablespoons chopped chives
½ teaspoon freshly grated nutmeg
1 × 150g tub fresh soft goat's cheese
50g (2oz) mature Cheddar, grated
Salt and freshly ground black pepper

Preheat the oven to 200°C/180°C fan/Gas 6. Put a heavy baking tray in the oven to heat up. You will also need a 28cm (11in) flan tin.

Measure the flour, butter, thyme and some pepper into a food processor or bowl. Process or rub together with your fingertips until the mixture resembles breadcrumbs.

Spoon in 5 level tablespoons of the soured cream then process or mix again just as long as it takes for the ingredients to come together. Turn out on to a lightly floured work surface and roll out to a circle about 5cm (2in) larger than the top diameter of the tin. Line the tin with the pastry then put it in the freezer.

Heat the oil in a large frying pan, then stir in the onions. Cook over a moderate heat, stirring frequently. Add the brown sugar and balsamic vinegar, fry for a minute then cover, lower the heat and cook for about 15 minutes, until softened and coloured. Remove the pan from the heat and leave aside to become cold.

Line the pastry with baking parchment and weight with baking beans. Place on the baking tray and bake for 10 minutes, then remove the paper and beans and continue to bake for a further 10 minutes. Remove the flan tin, leaving the baking tray in the oven. Turn the oven temperature down to 180°C/160°C fan/Gas 4.

The baked pastry shell and the filling can be made 24 hours in advance. The filling can be kept covered in the fridge for up to 8 hours.

If you can bear being parted from the flan tin, the freshly baked and cooled flan can be sealed inside a double thickness of plastic bags, all the air removed and sealed. Seal and label, then freeze for up to 4 months. To reheat, cover with foil and put in a cool oven at 150°C/140°C fan/ Gas 2 for 15 minutes just to warm through. The filled uncooked tart can also be frozen and then baked from frozen.

There's no need to bake the pastry blind; bake the complete tart on the floor of the roasting oven for about 30 minutes. If it is getting too brown, slide the cold sheet on to the second set of runners.

Combine the remaining soured cream with the eggs, chives and nutmeg in a bowl. Beat with a balloon whisk until smooth. Pour into the pan containing the onions and stir in half the goat's cheese, crumbled into soft lumps. Taste and season with salt and pepper, then pour into the pastry shell.

Sprinkle with the remaining crumbled goat's cheese and the Cheddar, then return to the oven to bake on the baking tray for a further 25–30 minutes. When baked, the tart should be gently puffed up and browned. Serve warm.

Tomato & Beef Curry with Coriander Naan

A curry is an excellent way to feed a crowd. Here is one that makes use of a wonderful cheap and flavoursome cut of meat to make an ideal party curry that is not overpoweringly strong, that looks rich and authentic and yet is surprisingly easy to make. This curry will actually improve with age – cool the cooked curry quickly and store in the fridge to 'mature'. For 12 people allow at least 450g (1lb) of rice.

SERVES 10–12

4 tablespoons sunflower oil

4 large onions, chopped

4 fat garlic cloves, crushed

A piece of fresh ginger root the size of a large walnut, peeled and grated

4–6 level tablespoons medium curry powder

2 × 227g tins peeled tomatoes

4 rounded tablespoons tomato purée

1.8kg (4lb) diced braising beef or cubed beef skirt

salt

600ml (1 pint) water

For the coriander naan bread

4 naan breads

175g (6oz) butter

2 garlic cloves, finely chopped

8 tablespoons chopped fresh coriander

FREEZE

Pack the cooled curry into a plastic freezer container or a double thickness of freezer bags. Seal, label and freeze for up to 2 months.

Heat the oil in a large pan and stir in the onions. Cook over a low heat for about 25–30 minutes until golden and soft.

Stir in the garlic and ginger, followed by the curry powder and carry on cooking for a further 3–4 minutes. Now add the tomatoes and tomato purée, then the meat. Stir, then cover and cook for 15 minutes. Uncover, add the salt and water and bring to the boil.

Adjust the heat to a gentle simmer, cover and cook for about 2 ½ hours or until the meat is tender, then check the seasoning. Alternatively, the curry can be cooked in a low oven at 160°C/140°C fan/Gas 3 for the same amount of time.

To prepare the bread, spread one side of each naan bread generously with butter. Sprinkle the butter surfaces with the garlic and coriander, then stack them together and wrap in a neat, leakproof foil packet. Bake at 200°C/180°C fan/Gas 6 for about 10-15 minutes, separate the breads and cut each one into three, then serve with the hot curry.

PREPARE AHEAD

The curry can be made, cooled, covered and stored in the fridge for up to 3 days. The bread can be prepared, wrapped in foil and kept in the fridge for up to 1 day. Reheat in a preheated oven at 200°C/180°C fan/Gas 6 for 20–30 minutes, removing the lid for the last 10 minutes.

AGA

Cook the curry in the simmering oven for about 3 hours until tender. The naan will take about 30 minutes in the same oven.

Orange Smoked Gammon with Orange & Chilli Salsa

This is an ideal meal to serve when cooking for a crowd. Serve the gammon hot or cold with Whipped Potatoes and Mixed Platter of Vegetables or a Dressed Mixed Leaf Salad (see pages 114, 136 and 148).

SERVES 10–12

2kg (4.4lb) smoked gammon joint

600ml (1 pint) orange juice from a carton

4 heaped tablespoons orange marmalade

For the orange and chilli salsa

1 red chilli, deseeded and chopped finely

2 oranges, skinned, segmented
    and finely chopped

1 small ripe mango, finely chopped

4 heaped tablespoons marmalade

2 tablespoons white wine vinegar

1 teaspoon finely grated fresh ginger root

A few drops of Tabasco sauce

Salt and freshly ground black pepper

PREPARE AHEAD
Gammon can be cooked and roasted up to 4 days ahead. The salsa can be made up to 2 days ahead.

AGA
Bring the gammon to the boil on the boiling plate, cover and transfer to the simmering oven for 2½ hours, or until tender. Brown in the roasting oven for 15 minutes.

Sit the gammon in a deep saucepan (large enough so a lid can be fitted). Pour in the orange juice and top up with water until the gammon is completely covered. Cover with the lid.

Bring to the boil for a couple of minutes, lower the heat and simmer very gently for 2½ hours. Alternatively, cook in the oven at 160°C/140°C fan/Gas 3 for 2½ hours or until tender.

While the ham is cooking, make the salsa. Tip all the ingredients into a bowl and season with salt and pepper. Set aside to marinate for up to 2 hours.

When the ham is cooked, remove it from the cooking liquid and, using a small sharp knife, carefully cut off the skin, leaving a thin layer of fat over the joint. Set aside to cool a little.

Turn up the oven to 220°C/200°C fan/Gas 7. Score the fat with a sharp knife. Line a small roasting tin with foil and sit the joint on top. Cover the ends of the ham with foil so they do not dry out and only the fat on top is showing. Spread the marmalade over the fat.

Roast for about 15–20 minutes or until golden and bubbling on top. Carve the ham and serve the salsa alongside.

Nasi Goreng with Tiger Prawn Kebabs

This Indonesian rice dish is a very good way to use up cooked rice or the last of a roast chicken. If you boil the rice specially for the recipe, do it the day before then keep it in the fridge overnight. The idea of serving the dish with prawn kebabs came from a trip to Australia and it works very well for a party.

SERVES 10–12

For the nasi goreng

450g (1lb) parboiled or easy-cook long-grain rice
9 rashers of smoked streaky bacon, rinded and chopped
Approx. 8 tablespoons olive oil
3 large onions, chopped
4 garlic cloves, crushed
½ teaspoon chilli powder
3 heaped teaspoons medium curry powder
3 boneless, skinless chicken breasts, cubed
9 tablespoons dark soy sauce
8 spring onions, chopped
500g pack of frozen, raw large tiger prawns
3 tablespoons French Dressing
   (see page 148)

For the omelettes

3 eggs, beaten
Salt and freshly ground black pepper
A little butter

To serve

Prawn crackers
A crisp green salad
A bowl of salted peanuts

Bring a large pan of generously salted water to the boil (see the instructions on the rice packet for the quantity of water). Stir in the rice, then cover and simmer for 12–15 minutes until tender. Drain the rice in a large sieve and rinse well by holding the sieve under the hot tap. Turn into a large bowl, cool and cover.

To make the omelettes, beat the eggs with a little salt and pepper in a bowl. Heat a large, empty frying pan, add a nut of butter, then use half the egg mix to make a thin, flat omelette. Turn it out on to a board to cool, then make another omelette with the remaining mixture and leave to cool. Roll the 2 omelettes together and shred in fine strips. Put on a plate, cover and leave aside until ready to use.

Heat a large, deep, non-stick frying pan. Sprinkle in the bacon and heat until the fat runs. Pour in the olive oil then, when hot, stir in the onions and garlic. Cover and cook over a low heat for about 20 minutes or until softened but not coloured.

Now stir in the chilli and curry powders and cook for a few minutes before stirring in the chicken. Cover and cook for about 5 minutes, then uncover and add the soy sauce and the rice. Taste and season with salt and pepper.

Arrange in a shallow dish. Finally, sprinkle over the shredded omelette and spring onions. Stir well, cover and keep warm in a low oven. Preheat the grill to maximum.

The rice part of the dish can be made, omitting the addition of the shredded omelette and chopped spring onions. It can be kept covered in the fridge for up to 2 days. To reheat, spread the rice mixture in a buttered shallow ovenproof dish (or two) and put in a preheated oven at 200°C/180°C fan/Gas 6 for 30 minutes, stirring from time to time, to heat and get crisp. Fork in the onion and decorate with shredded omelette and cook just sufficiently to warm through, about another 5 minutes.

AGA
Cook on the boiling plate. To reheat, slide the dish on to the second set of runners in the roasting oven for 20–25 minutes. Cook kebabs in the top of the roasting oven for about 6 minutes in all.

While the grill is heating, thread the prawns on to short skewers; there should be sufficient to serve three prawns per person. Arrange them on a foil-lined grill pan and brush with the French dressing. Grill for about 2–3 minutes, then turn, brush with more dressing and grill until pink and cooked.

Arrange the prawn kebabs on top of the rice, arrange the prawn crackers around the dish and serve with a bowl of dressed salad and a bowl of salted peanuts.

TIP
Allow 25–50 g (1–2oz) rice per person, so for 12 people use 350–450 g (12oz–1lb). It can be prepared ahead; to reheat plain boiled rice, put in a lightly buttered, shallow dish, cover with lightly buttered foil, then reheat in a preheated oven at 180°C/160 °C fan/Gas 4.

Roast Fillet of Beef with Herbed Horseradish Sauce

Fillet of beef is a real treat, and here it is served with a tarragon-horseradish sauce. This recipe is really quick and easy to make for a perfect dinner with friends.

SERVES 8–10

1kg (2.2lb) middle cut of fillet of beef
Olive oil
2 tablespoons black peppercorns,
   crushed
Salt

For the sauce
1 × 200g tub full-fat crème fraîche
2 tablespoons chopped tarragon
2 tablespoons chopped parsley
Juice of ½ a lemon
6 tablespoons light mayonnaise
2 tablespoons hot horseradish sauce
A dash of caster sugar
Salt and freshly ground black pepper

Preheat the oven to 220°C/200°C fan/Gas 7.

Rub the beef fillet with oil. Scatter the crushed peppercorns on a board and roll the fillet in them. Sprinkle with salt.

Heat a frying pan until very hot. Brown the fillet on all sides until sealed and golden brown. Transfer to a small roasting tin and roast in the preheated oven for 20 minutes for medium rare – rest before carving.

To make the sauce, measure all the ingredients into a bowl, season with salt and pepper and mix to combine.

Carve the beef into thin slices and serve with the sauce.

PREPARE AHEAD
To serve cold, the beef can be roasted 2 days ahead; carve just before serving otherwise the beef will discolour. To serve hot, brown the beef up to 12 hours ahead and roast to serve. The sauce can be made up to 2 days ahead; the flavours will be stronger the longer it is left.

AGA
Roast on the second set of runners in the roasting oven for 20 minutes.

Salmon & Broccoli Fish Pie

A Scandinavian-inspired and very upmarket fish pie.

SERVES 10

For the topping

1.1kg (2½lb) potatoes,
    peeled and cubed
A generous knob of butter
Approx. 100ml (3 ½ fl oz) milk
Salt and freshly ground
    black pepper

For the filling

50g (2oz) butter
1 large onion, roughly chopped
50g (2oz) plain flour
600ml (1 pint) hot milk
Juice of ½ a lemon
100g mature Cheddar cheese, grated
500g (1lb 2oz) salmon fillet, skinned
    and cut into 1cm (½-in) pieces
4 hard-boiled eggs, quartered
225g (8oz) broccoli, broken into
    small sprigs

TIP

It is a strange thing to say but don't buy eggs too fresh when you need to hard-boil them. Nowadays they can be so fresh, they are impossible to peel, so use week-old eggs for hard-boiling.

Grease a shallow, 2-litre (4-pint) shallow dish.

To make the topping, cook the potatoes in boiling salted water until they are completely tender. Drain in a colander.

Add the butter and milk to the hot pan and return to the heat until bubbling. Return the potatoes to the pan, remove from the heat, mash, and season to taste. Cover and put aside until ready to use.

Next, make the sauce for the filling. Melt the butter in a medium-sized pan, stir in the onion and cook over a low heat until softened but not coloured. Sprinkle in the flour and cook for 1 minute, then pull the pan aside from the heat before gradually stirring in the milk. Allow to thicken.

Return the pan to the heat and bring to the boil, stirring. Lower the heat to a gentle simmer and add the lemon juice, half the cheese and then the salmon pieces. Season and remove from the heat and pour into the dish. Arrange the eggs over the top, cover and leave to cool.

Cook the broccoli in boiling salted water for 4 minutes. Immediately drain in a colander and cool under cold running water. Drain well, dry on kitchen paper then arrange the broccoli in an even layer over the eggs, pressing the broccoli down a little into the sauce.

Spread the mash over the top and sprinkle
with the remaining cheese. Cover and chill
for 1–2 hours until firm.

Preheat the oven to 180°C/160°C fan/Gas 4.
Bake the pie for 30–35 minutes or until crisp
and golden. Serve at once; if kept hot for long
the colour of the broccoli will fade.

Mediterranean Tuna en Croûte

This is a good family supper using fairly standard store-cupboard ingredients. It's very popular with the young, and inexpensive to make.

SERVES 8–10

4 × 200g tins tuna chunks in oil
2 garlic cloves, crushed
1 medium onion, cut into large chunks
175g (6oz) button mushrooms, quartered
1 × 400g tin chopped tomatoes
2 tablespoons tomato purée
1 red pepper, deseeded and sliced
    into very thin strips
2 tablespoons chopped fresh basil
2 teaspoons sugar
75g (3oz) pitted black olives, halved
Salt and freshly ground black pepper
1 × 350g pack frozen puff pastry,
    thawed
1 × 50g tin anchovies, drained
    and chopped
1 egg, beaten

You will need a baking tray, greased or lined with baking parchment.

Drain the tuna in a sieve set over a bowl. Take 2 tablespoons of the drained oil and heat it in a large frying pan. Stir in the garlic and onion, then cover and cook over a low heat for about 10–15 minutes or until softened and slightly coloured.

Add the mushrooms and continue to cook for a further 5 minutes before adding the tomatoes and tomato purée. Turn up the heat and cook briskly until most of the pan juices have evaporated.

Add the drained tuna, the pepper, basil, sugar, olives and salt and pepper. Heat just sufficiently to make sure most of the liquid has evaporated, being careful not to stir too vigorously and break up the peppers and tuna too much. Cover and leave aside to become cold.

Roll out the pastry very thinly on a floured surface to about 38 × 33cm (15 × 13in). Trim the edges to make a neat rectangle and reserve the pastry trimmings. Transfer the pastry to the baking tray.

Put the cold filling down the centre of the pastry in a band 13–15cm (5–6in) wide, leaving a 5cm (2in) border free at each short end. Scatter the chopped anchovies over the top of the filling and brush the edges of the pastry with beaten egg. Fold the two short ends in over the filling and bring the long sides up to meet down the middle of the filling. Crimp the edges together firmly between thumb and forefinger.

Once the pie has been made, do not glaze but cover with clingfilm and keep in the fridge for up to 12 hours before baking, then glaze and follow the recipe.

FREEZE
Carefully wrap the unbaked pie in foil, seal and label, then freeze for up to 1 month.

AGA
Bake on the grid shelf on the lowest set of runners in the roasting oven for about 25 minutes until golden brown. Slide the baking tray on to the floor of the oven for a further 10 minutes to crisp the base and, if necessary, slide the cold plain shelf in to prevent the top from getting too brown.

Brush the pie all over with beaten egg. Roll out the pastry trimming and cut into long thin strips. Lay the strips diagonally both ways across the surface, making a lattice. Brush the strips with egg then cover with clingfilm and place in the fridge for a few hours to firm up.

Preheat the oven to 220°C/200°C fan/Gas 7.

Uncover and bake the pie for about 25–30 minutes, or until golden brown.

Quick Cassoulet-style Sausages & Beans

A proper French cassoulet is a magnificent dish, taking days to make in a very large casserole; a dish you might try to do properly once in a lifetime. By contrast, this recipe retains all the elements of good home cooking on a much more modest scale, using everyday ingredients.

SERVES 10–12

350g (12oz) dried haricot beans, soaked overnight
3 tablespoons sunflower oil
350g (12oz) smoked streaky bacon, rinded and cut into strips
350g (12oz) smallish onions, quartered
2 tablespoons plain flour
2 × 400g tins chopped tomatoes
2–3 tablespoons tomato purée
2 bay leaves
3 sprigs of fresh thyme
Salt and freshly ground black pepper
20 Toulouse or other French sausages

To garnish
Chopped fresh parsley

Drain the beans and put them in a pan with plenty of water to cover. Bring to the boil, then adjust the heat to a gentle simmer and cook for 30 minutes or until the beans are tender. Drain, reserving the cooking liquor.

Heat the oil in a large pan and fry the bacon until just beginning to crisp. Stir in the onions and continue to cook until the pieces start to brown around the edges. Sprinkle in the flour, stir and cook for a minute before adding the tomatoes, tomato purée, bay leaves and thyme.

Add the cooked beans and 250ml (8fl oz) of the reserved liquor. Bring the mixture to the boil and add a little more bean liquor if you prefer, then taste and season with salt and pepper. Preheat the oven to 200°C/180°C fan/Gas 6.

Pour the bean mixture into a large shallow baking dish, and arrange the sausages on top. Cover with foil and bake for 20 minutes. Remove the foil and bake for a further 20 minutes, turning the sausages once until the sausages are browned and the beans piping hot. Scatter with parsley and serve.

PREPARE AHEAD
The bean mixture can be made, cooled, covered and kept in the fridge for up to 3 days. If you keep it this long, add a further 150ml (5fl oz) of bean liquor. Reheat as per the recipe.

AGA
Cook, covered, on the grid shelf on the floor of the roasting oven for 15 minutes. Then uncover for a further 10–15 minutes, turning the sausages to brown.

TIP
If time is short and soaking pulses overnight is not possible, put them in a pan with plenty of cold water to cover, bring to the boil then remove from the heat, cover and leave to stand for 1 hour. Cover with fresh water and press on with the recipe.

Steak & Kidney Pie

If you have a flameproof casserole then all the frying and cooking can be done in the one pot. If not, use a frying pan then transfer the ingredients to a larger pan to cook. Make two pies for a party or double up if you have a larger pie dish. Preferably, start this dish the day before it is served.

SERVES 8–10

For the filling

900g (2lb) beef skirt

450g (1lb) beef kidneys,
    cores removed

50g (2oz) plain flour

1 teaspoon salt

Freshly ground black pepper

Approx. 5 tablespoons sunflower oil

2 large onions, chopped

175g (6oz) smoked streaky bacon,
    rinded and cut in strips

300ml (10fl oz) red wine

300ml (10fl oz) Beef Stock
    (see page 248)

225g (8oz) brown chestnut
    mushrooms

For the topping

500g (1lb) puff pastry

1 egg

Salt

You will need either a shallow, rectangular pie dish, preferably one that is 28 × 23cm (11 × 9in), with a 5mm (¼in) wide rim and 1.5-litre (2½-pint) capacity. Alternatively, use a 23cm (9in) round, shallow dish of the same capacity.

Cube the beef, then cut the cored kidneys in thick slices. Mix the measured flour and salt with plenty of pepper.

Heat a couple of tablespoons of the oil in a flameproof casserole or frying pan. Toss about a third of the meat in the seasoned flour, then fry over a moderate to high heat until evenly browned. Use a slotted spoon to remove it to a plate, then flour and fry the next batch in the same manner, adding a little more oil to the casserole when it is needed. Continue in this way until all the meat and kidneys have been browned.

Now stir in the onions and bacon and cook over a low to moderate heat for 10 minutes or until lightly browned. Stir in any remaining seasoned flour and cook for a further 5 minutes, allowing the flour time to brown. Gradually stir in the red wine and stock and bring to simmering point.

Return the meat and kidneys to the casserole with any juices, then cover and cook over a low heat for about 2 hours or until the meat is tender. Add the mushrooms to the casserole, cover and cook for a further 15 minutes, then remove from the heat and leave to cool. Chill overnight, ready to make the pie the following day.

The meat filling can be cooked and kept in the fridge for up to 2 days. The pastry-covered but unglazed pie can be covered with clingfilm and kept in the fridge for up to 1 day. Allow the pie to come up to room temperature before glazing and baking following the recipe.

FREEZE
Open freeze the pastry-covered uncooked pie, then cover with foil, seal, label and freeze for up to 2 months.

AGA
Stand the pie dish in a roasting tin. Cook in the roasting oven, on the lowest set of runners, for about 30 minutes or until golden. Then slide the cold plain shelf above and continue cooking until bubbling hot.

Preheat the oven to 200°C/180°C fan/Gas 6.

Place a handle-less cup or pie funnel in the centre of the pie dish in order to support the pastry and spoon in the cold meat mixture around it.

Roll the pastry out to a size that is about 2.5cm (1in) larger than the top of the pie and about the thickness of a pound coin. Beat the egg with a generous pinch of salt, then brush this on the rim of the dish. Cut a strip from around the outside of the pastry and press this on to the rim of the dish. Brush the pastry strip with more beaten egg, then cover the pie with the remaining sheet of pastry, pressing the edges together all around the rim.

Trim away the excess pastry from the rim, then pinch the edges together to form a tight seal so no juices can escape. Re-roll any pastry trimmings to decorate the pie if you wish, then glaze all over with beaten egg. Make a steam hole in the centre.

Transfer to a baking tray and bake in the oven for about 35 minutes or until the pie is a pale golden brown. Now lower the oven temperature to 180°C/160°C fan/Gas 4 and continue baking for about 15 minutes or until the pie is piping hot and perfectly browned. Serve immediately.

Danish-style Open Sandwiches

It can seem a daunting task to produce a large quantity of sandwiches to feed a group. My answer is to make the Danish-style smörrebrod, as they call it, or open sandwich. This style of bread base with a variety of ingredients arranged on top gives a very attractive-looking sandwich, with not too much bread. The Danes use mostly a range of rye breads for the sandwich bases, but this can be adapted according to the occasion, available breads, and your tastes.

If the occasion is one where people are able to sit and eat, then thinly sliced bread can be served with quite elaborate toppings, to be eaten with a knife and fork.

But the basic idea works just as well should guests be standing and eating out of doors. For this, you would need a firmer bread base, such as pieces of halved French baguette, and a less elaborate topping that will stay in place while it is eaten. Just see that your guests are well supplied with generous-sized napkins so that no cutlery or plates are needed.

CHOOSE YOUR BASE

For a light lunch, use the denser types of bread that will slice thinly, such as light, medium or dark rye bread, pumpernickel, grain or granary breads.

For outside eating, use a more robust, thicker bread. Brown and white baguettes, sliced in half lengthways and cut into 9–10cm chunks are ideal. Small pitta breads, or larger ones (halved) are also good; some types are available cut open into a neat pocket and so are easier to prepare.

SPREADS

There are alternatives to using butter; try low-calorie mayonnaise or low-fat yoghurt or light cream cheese. A soft goat's cheese, pesto, sundried tomato paste, mango chutney, olive tapenade or grainy mustard will add lots of flavour to your sandwiches.

The sandwiches can be prepared in the morning, assembled on the trays with all but the final garnishes, such as sliced lemon or coriander, to add. Cover the trays with clingfilm and chill. They will keep for up to 4 hours. Just before serving, add the final garnishes to the sandwiches and decorate the trays with fresh herbs, lemon and salad leaves.

TOPPINGS

If you can, find out how many people you're feeding and allow three sandwiches per person and offer three different types of open sandwich. Choose toppings with a mixture of colours, because you will see the whole filling. These can be anything you choose, but here are some of my favourites:

1 A spread of basil pesto, topped with sliced mozzarella, sliced tomatoes, black olives and fresh basil, drizzled with French Dressing (page 148).

2 A spread of lemon-sharp mayonnaise topped with slices of smoked salmon, garnished with paper-thin slices of lemon and fresh dill.

3 Slices of Cambazola cheese with seedless black grapes and flat-leaf parsley.

4 Prawns mixed with a little herb-flavoured mayonnaise, arranged on lettuce leaves and topped with thin slices of lemon.

5 Rare roast beef with horseradish and rocket leaves, garnished with thin slices of pickled cucumber.

See also page 253 for some general advice on bread, spread and filling quantities.

SOMETHING ON THE SIDE

*

Bakes, chargrills & posh salads

I THINK ACCOMPANYING VEGETABLES should always looks attractive, and should be fresh and lightly cooked. You don't need a full recipe for this, but I have given here something that I've often demonstrated at my Aga classes: a Mixed Platter of Vegetables (page 136). It uses the chef's technique of blanching the vegetables in advance, then cooking and refreshing them in cold water before a fast reheat to serve. The blanching and refreshing can be done the day before so that they just need heating through quickly in the oven. Vegetables cooked this way will retain their colour and crunch.

Instead of potato, there is Celeriac au Gratin (page 140), which is just as delicious, even without the usual rich cream. There is a wonderfully, bright green couscous, which is a perfect side for a summery barbecue or alfresco lunch. And there is also my trusted recipe for Whipped Potatoes (page 144), which I've included here as a simple reminder of how delicious well-made, mashed potatoes can be.

These recipes shouldn't be limited to an accompanying role only – any of these recipes would make a good lunch, particularly the Spicy Mexican Bean Salad (page 150) or the Chorizo, Avocado & Tomato Salad (page 153). Others would be good to serve at a buffet-style dinner and can be easily doubled to stretch further.

And don't forget that a couple of the first courses in Chapter 1 could also be served as an accompaniment, too.

Maple-roasted Root Vegetables

These are sweet, herby and divine! Try with Fast-roasted Lamb with Lemon & Thyme (page 98) and Chicken with Vermouth & Sage (page 95).

SERVES 4–6

500g (1lb 2oz) butternut squash, peeled, cut in half and seeds removed

2 large sweet potatoes, peeled

3 large parsnips, peeled

3 tablespoons olive oil

Salt and freshly ground black pepper

1 tablespoon maple syrup

1 teaspoon finely chopped thyme leaves

Preheat the oven to 240°C/220°C fan/Gas 8. Cut the squash, potatoes and parsnips into 2cm (1in) cubes.

Measure the oil into a large roasting tin and heat in the oven for 3 minutes until piping hot. Add the vegetables, season with salt and pepper and toss in the oil. Return to the oven and roast for 30 minutes.

Add the maple syrup and thyme, turn over and return to the oven for 5–10 minutes or until glazed and golden. Serve hot.

PREPARE AHEAD
To prevent the vegetables from discolouring, blanch in boiling water for 1 minute, drain, then refresh in cold water and set aside until needed – this can be done up to 12 hours ahead.

AGA
Roast on the floor of the roasting oven, as above.

Aromatic Rice

This flavoured rice is perfect with any Thai or Indian recipe, such as Monkfish & Prawn Curry (page 83) and Quick Chicken Curry (page 48).

SERVES 4–6

100g (4oz) French beans, sliced
    into 5mm (¼in) pieces
2 tablespoons olive oil
1 large onion, finely chopped
2 garlic cloves, crushed
½ red chilli, deseeded and diced
350g (12oz) long-grain rice
1 teaspoon ground cumin
600ml (1 pint) Chicken Stock
    (see page 248)
A small bunch of coriander, chopped
Juice of 1 lemon or lime
Salt and freshly ground black pepper

Cook the French beans in boiling salted water until just cooked.

Heat the oil in a large saucepan, add the onion, garlic and chilli and fry for a few minutes until starting to soften.

Rinse the rice in cold water, drain and add to the pan. Sprinkle in the cumin and fry for a minute. Pour in the stock, bring to the boil, stirring, cover and simmer over a very low heat for 10 minutes or until the rice is cooked.

Add the cooked beans, coriander and lemon or lime juice. Season with salt and pepper and serve hot or cold.

PREPARE AHEAD
If serving the rice cold it can be cooked up to 8 hours ahead.

AGA
Bring the rice to the boil, cover and transfer to the simmering oven for 10–15 minutes or until the rice is cooked.

Leek & Potato Gratin

The great advantage of this potato dish is that the main part of the cooking can be done several hours ahead. This can be useful sometimes, if only to free the oven for other things. After the topping is added, the dish has a final short bake and emerges a melting, golden mass of creamy potatoes and cheese. Serve this with Whole Roasted Garlic Chicken instead of roast potatoes (page 40).

SERVES 6

225g (8oz) leeks, trimmed

900g (2lb) potatoes

40g (1½oz) butter

1 teaspoon salt

Freshly ground black pepper

Freshly grated nutmeg

300ml (10fl oz) Chicken Stock
  (see page 248) or vegetable stock

4 tablespoons double cream

40g (1½oz) Gruyère, grated

PREPARE AHEAD
Bake the potatoes until cooked, then remove from the oven and cover. They can be kept at room temperature for up to 4 hours. When ready, add the cream and cheese, then follow the recipe above.

Preheat the oven to 200°C/180°C fan/Gas 6. You will need a shallow, ovenproof dish about 20 × 28cm (8 × 11in), buttered. Finely slice the leeks, wash well and drain. Peel the potatoes and slice thinly using a mandolin, in a food processor fitted with the thin cutting disc, or with a sharp knife.

Melt the butter in a large, deep frying pan and stir in the prepared leeks. Cook over a moderate heat for about 2 minutes. Add the sliced potatoes and sprinkle with the salt, a generous amount of pepper and grated nutmeg. Stir well to mix then turn into the prepared dish.

Spread the potato mixture evenly, then pour in the stock. Bake for 45 minutes or until the potatoes are cooked, then remove the dish from the oven. Reset the oven temperature to 220°C/200°C fan/Gas 7.

Pour the cream over the potatoes then sprinkle with the cheese. Replace the dish near the top of the oven to reheat and brown. This will take about 20 minutes if the potatoes are hot, about 30 minutes if the dish was cold.

AGA
Bake on the grid shelf on the floor of the roasting oven for about 45 minutes. The potatoes should be just tender and most of the stock absorbed. After adding the cream and cheese, raise the shelf to the highest position and bake for a further 20 minutes or until golden brown. Add an extra 10 minutes or so if the gratin was cold when returned to the oven.

Mixed Platter of Vegetables

The perfect prepare-ahead vegetable recipe. Serve this with Classic Duck with Crisp Sage & Onion (page 60) or The Best Cod & Herb Fishcakes (page 89) for a complete meal.

SERVES 6

500g (1lb 2oz) celeriac, peeled

500g (1lb 2oz) King Edward potatoes, peeled

350g (12oz) baby carrots, peeled

2 leeks, sliced into 2cm (1in) slices

225g (8oz) cauliflower, cut into even-sized florets

225g (8oz) broccoli, cut into even-sized florets

50g (1oz) butter, softened

6 tablespoons full-fat crème fraîche

Salt and freshly ground black pepper

PREPARE AHEAD

The dish can be made up to a day ahead and kept in the fridge. Once the platter of vegetables is reheated, serve it at once – otherwise the broccoli will lose its colour and the other veg will lose their flavour.

AGA

Bake on the second set of runners in the roasting oven for 25 minutes.

Preheat the oven to 200°C/180°C fan/Gas 6 for 25 minutes. Butter a large, flat ovenproof platter or dish.

Cut the celeriac and potatoes into 4cm (2in) cubes. Put them in a pan of cold salted water and boil for 15–20 minutes or until tender. Drain well.

Bring another pan of salted water to the boil. Add the carrots and boil for 8 minutes or until tender. Using a slotted spoon, scoop out the carrots and refresh in cold water. Add the leeks and boil for 7 minutes, scoop out and refresh in cold water. Bring back to the boil, add the cauliflower and broccoli and boil for 4 minutes, drain and refresh in cold water.

Whizz the celeriac and potatoes in a processor until smooth. Add the butter and crème fraîche, season with salt and pepper and whizz again until smooth.

Arrange the leeks in a row at one end of the dish. Arrange the carrots next to the leeks, spoon on the potato and celeriac purée and finish with the broccoli and cauliflower, so you have neat rows of each vegetable. Cover with buttered foil.

Bake in the preheated oven for 25 minutes or until piping hot. Remove the foil and serve.

Glazed Onions

Glazed sweet roasted onions, perfect to serve with a roast, such as Butterflied Lamb in Lemon Marinade (page 76) or Lamb Paysanne & Spinach Stuffing (page 94).

SERVES 6–8

50g (2oz) butter, melted

Salt and freshly ground black pepper

3 large, mild Spanish onions, halved

1 tablespoon white wine vinegar

½ teaspoon salt

½ teaspoon mustard powder

2 tablespoons soft brown sugar

1 teaspoon mild paprika

PREPARE AHEAD

Have the onions ready to roast. They can be kept, covered, in the fridge for up to 8 hours before roasting.

AGA

Roast on the grid shelf on the floor of the roasting oven for about 35 minutes. If the onions are getting too brown and are not yet tender, slide the cold plain shelf above the onions.

Preheat the oven to 180°C/160°C fan/Gas 4. You will need a baking dish or tin the right size to take six onion halves.

Brush the base of the dish with a little of the melted butter and season with salt and pepper. Arrange the halved onions in the prepared dish, cut-side down.

Combine the remaining ingredients in a bowl and spoon over the onions. Cover and roast for 45–50 minutes or until the onions are tender when pierced with a skewer.

Cauliflower, Broccoli & Potato Bake

Delicious served on its own, this bake is also great with sausages and chops, such as Barnsley Chops on page 51 or Quick Cassoulet-style Sausage and Beans on page 122.

SERVES 6

500g (1lb 2oz) potatoes, peeled
    and cut into 2cm (¾-in) cubes
1 large onion, roughly chopped
350g (12oz) cauliflower florets
250g (9oz) broccoli florets

For the cheese sauce
50g (2oz) butter
50g (2oz) plain flour
600ml (1 pint) milk, warmed
Salt and freshly ground black pepper
1 teaspoon Dijon mustard
75g (3oz) Parmesan, grated
75g (3oz) mature Cheddar, grated

PREPARE AHEAD
The whole dish can be made up to 12 hours ahead and kept in the fridge.

AGA
Bake on the second set of runners in the roasting oven for 20 minutes.

Preheat the oven 220°C/200°C fan/Gas 7. You will also need a 2-litre (3-pint) shallow ovenproof dish, buttered.

Bring a large saucepan of salted water to the boil. Add the potato and onion, bring back to the boil and boil for 4 minutes. Add the cauliflower and broccoli and boil for a further 4 minutes or until the vegetables are just cooked. Drain and refresh in cold water to stop the cooking.

To make the sauce, melt the butter in a pan, add the flour and whisk over heat for 1 minute. Gradually add the warm milk, whisking until the sauce is thickened and smooth. Season with salt and pepper. Add the mustard and half both the Parmesan and Cheddar.

Make sure the vegetables are dry and arrange in the buttered dish. Season with salt and pepper, pour over the cheese sauce and sprinkle with the remaining cheeses.

Bake in the oven for 20–25 minutes until lightly golden and bubbling.

Celeriac au Gratin

Celeriac is the Cinderella of the vegetable world. Although it made its appearance in Britain at the same time as broccoli, it has never caught on to the same extent, although it is completely delicious. Its mild celery flavour goes particularly well with potatoes. Usually the two vegetables are mashed together and served with game stews, but just for a change I decided to do a gratin and the result was as good as, if not better. Try this with Pheasant Normandy-style (see page 99).

SERVES 5–6

1 tablespoon lemon juice

2 medium celeriac roots

300ml (10fl oz) Chicken Stock
(see page 248) or vegetable stock

Salt and freshly ground black pepper

40g (1½oz) fresh white breadcrumbs

40g (1½oz) Parmesan, freshly grated

Preheat the oven to 220°C/200°C fan/Gas 7. Butter an oval gratin dish (about 28cm/11in long) and sprinkle it with some salt and pepper.

Have ready a pan of cold salted water mixed with the lemon juice. Peel the celeriac thickly, then cut in quarters. Slice each quarter into slices about 3mm (1/8 in) thick. Immediately drop the slices into the cold water to prevent the vegetable discolouring.

Bring the water to the boil and simmer for 6 minutes. Drain the celeriac and arrange in the prepared gratin dish. Pour in the stock and season with salt and pepper. Combine the breadcrumbs and cheese and sprinkle evenly over the top.

Bake for 25–30 minutes or until the celeriac is tender when tested with a skewer. The top should be toasted, golden and crisp. Serve hot.

PREPARE AHEAD
Have the parboiled celeriac ready in the dish, minus the cheese and breadcrumb topping. Cover and keep in the fridge for up to 6 hours. Add the topping just before baking, then follow the recipe above.

AGA
Bake on the second set of runners in the roasting oven for 20 minutes or until brown on top and the celeriac is tender.

Green Couscous Salad

Couscous has to be the best of all the 'instant' foods. It is semolina that has been rolled in flour, which means the grains stay separate when cooked. It is sold pre-treated to cook very quickly and easily. The recipe is ideal as an accompaniment to grilled kebabs, chicken or fish, such as Seafood Kebabs (page 82). To make it into more of a main course, you could add 150g (5oz) crumbled goat's or feta cheese. Also try with Maple-spiced Chicken (page 71).

SERVES 4 AS A MAIN COURSE
OR 6 AS A SIDE SALAD
250g (9oz) couscous
400ml (14fl oz) vegetable stock
150g (5oz) fresh asparagus spears
salt
Freshly ground black pepper
Juice of 1 lemon
4 tablespoons olive oil
6 spring onions, chopped
150g (5oz) mangetout peas,
    sliced on the diagonal
50g (2oz) pine nuts, toasted
6 tablespoons chopped flat-leaf parsley
3 tablespoons chopped mint

To garnish
Lemon slices
Sprigs of mint and parsley

Measure the couscous in to a large bowl. Bring the vegetable stock to the boil. Cut the asparagus spears into 2.5cm (1½in) lengths and add to the boiling stock with the mangetout.

Cook for about 3 minutes or until just tender but still with bite, then remove the pan from the heat. Position a colander over the bowl of couscous, then pour the liquid contents of the pan into it.

Add the salt and some pepper to the couscous, give it a stir then cover and leave aside to cool. Refresh the asparagus and mangetout under cold running water, drain, then pat dry on kitchen paper; leave aside until needed.

By this time, the couscous should have absorbed all the stock. Add the lemon juice and olive oil and toss with two forks to mix. Now add the spring onions, asparagus, mangetout, pine nuts, parsley and mint.

Toss again, then taste and flavour with more salt, pepper or lemon juice if preferred. Serve at room temperature, garnished with slices of lemon and sprigs of mint and parsley.

PREPARE AHEAD
The salad can be prepared without the garnish, cooled, covered and stored in the fridge for up to 6 hours. Not suitable for freezing.

Whipped Potatoes

You may wonder why I am giving a recipe for something as simple as mashed – or whipped – potatoes. Maybe it's because mashed potato is so simple to make that it is often cooked so badly. And yet when properly cooked, it is the most delicious and satisfying vegetable of all. It is important to start with the right sort of potatoes that mash well, such as King Edwards, Golden Wonder, Desirée or Wilja. These all have a mealy, floury texture that holds the air, butter and milk that are beaten into them in a light, fluffy consistency. Never attempt to mash new potatoes or anything that is described as a salad potato. These will have a compact, waxy texture that will only ever produce a nasty, gluey, lumpish mess. By the way, do consider buying a potato ricer – a bit like a huge garlic crusher – you won't regret it. Serve this with Barnsley Chops with Onion Gravy (page 51), Paprika Chicken (page 47) and Pheasant Casserole with Thyme & Prunes (page 96) – any dishes with a rich sauce you can soak up with the potato.

SERVES 6–8
1.25kg (2½lb) old, floury potatoes
Salt and freshly ground black pepper
Approx. 250ml (8fl oz) milk
100g (4oz) butter, plus extra to serve

Because they are to be boiled in their skins, scrub the potatoes and, if large, halve or quarter them. Try to keep the pieces an even size so they cook in the same time. Put into a pan, cover with cold water and add about 2 teaspoons of salt.

Bring to the boil, then boil gently for about 30 minutes or until the potatoes feel absolutely tender when tested with a skewer. Drain, cool a little, then quickly remove the skins.

Add most of the milk and the butter to the pan and heat until bubbling. Now either press the potatoes through a sieve or a potato ricer into the pan. Beat the potatoes, adding more milk if necessary, until you have the ideal consistency to accompany the main course.

Taste and season with pepper and extra salt if needed. Spoon a soft drift of potatoes into a warmed serving dish and serve immediately topped with an extra knob of butter.

PREPARE AHEAD
Prepare the potatoes and spoon into a warmed serving dish. Cover with a butter paper then seal with foil and place in a cool oven at 140°C/120°C fan/Gas 1 for up to 1 hour. If oven space is not available, do as the chefs do and keep the potatoes hot in the top half of a double pan over hot water.

Roasted Mediterranean Vegetables

Serve cold as a salad, or hot without the balsamic vinegar and olives. You can also barbecue the vegetables, if you wish. Try with Mediterranean Tuna en Croûte (page 124) and Butterflied Lamb in Lemon Marinade (page 76).

SERVES 4–6
1 courgette
2 red peppers, deseeded
1 yellow pepper, deseeded
1 fennel bulb
4 garlic cloves, thinly sliced
1–2 tablespoons olive oil
Salt and freshly ground black pepper
2 teaspoons balsamic vinegar
   (if serving cold)
50g (2oz) pitted black olives in oil
   (if serving cold)
Fresh green salad leaves
   (if serving cold)

AGA
Spread the oiled vegetables over the base of a large roasting tin and cook on the floor of the roasting oven for 30 minutes until slightly charred.

Cut the courgette diagonally into 5mm (¼-in) slices. Cut each pepper into 5mm (¼-in) sticks. Trim the stalks of the fennel level with the bulb, then cut into wedges like a cake. Boil the fennel wedges in salted water for 5 minutes then drain. Put all the vegetables and garlic in a large bowl and combine with the oil and some salt and pepper.

Preheat the oven to 220°C/200°C fan/Gas 7 or the grill to maximum for 10 minutes. Arrange the vegetables on a baking tray or grill rack. Oven-roast the veg for 25 minutes or grill for about 10 minutes, turning once.

Serve the hot veg immediately or, to serve cold, allow the vegetables to cool, toss with balsamic vinegar and black olives and serve on a bed of fresh green salad leaves.

PREPARE AHEAD
If the vegetables are to be served hot they can be prepared and kept in a covered bowl in the fridge for up to 1 day. If they are to be served as a cold salad, they can be grilled or oven roasted, mixed with balsamic vinegar and olives and kept covered in the fridge for up to 2 days.

Posh Jacket Potatoes

These have a lovely filling to make a change from plain jacket potatoes.

SERVES 6–8

4 large baking potatoes

about 2 tablespoons milk

A knob of butter

3 tablespoons fresh pesto

75g (3oz) Parmesan, grated

100g (4oz) sun-blushed tomatoes, finely chopped

A little oil

Salt and freshly ground black pepper

2 tablespoons chopped parsley

PREPARE AHEAD
The potatoes can be filled and ready for their second bake up to 4 hours ahead. To reheat, roast at the same temperature for 30 minutes – you may need to cover with foil if the top is getting too brown.

AGA
Bake in the roasting oven for an hour or until soft. Once refilled, roast on the second set of runners for 15 minutes.

Preheat the oven to 220°C/200°C fan/Gas 7.

Put the potatoes in the oven and bake for about an hour or until soft in the middle.

Slice each potato in half and scoop out the soft centre into a bowl. Add the remaining ingredients (except the parsley) to the bowl, season with salt and pepper and mix to combine.

Spoon the mixture back into the skin then arrange the potatoes skin-side down in a roasting tin. Drizzle over any sun-blushed tomato oil or a little olive oil and return to the oven for 15 minutes or until golden and the skins are crisp.

Sprinkle with the chopped parsley and serve hot.

Dressed Mixed Leaf Salad

Vary green salads by adding different types of lettuces – seasonal leaves; young spinach leaves; lamb's lettuce (also known as corn salad); radicchio; some home-grown purslane; chicory; endive; and fresh, leafy herbs. I particularly like adding torn leaves of mint and chopped garlic chives. Serve with rich bakes, such as Red Pepper, Mushroom & Leek Lasagne (page 90) or summery tarts, such as Onion & Cheese Tart (page 110) for a light lunch.

SERVES 6–8

For the French dressing
1 tablespoon lemon juice
1 tablespoon white wine vinegar
1 teaspoon mustard powder
Salt and freshly ground black pepper
1 garlic clove, crushed
1 tablespoon caster sugar
2 tablespoons sunflower oil
1 tablespoon olive oil

For the salad
4 spring onions, shredded
4 celery sticks, diagonally cut
    in 5mm (¼in) slices
1 small fennel bulb, thinly sliced
½ small Webbs or iceberg lettuce
2 Little Gem lettuces
½ cucumber
A few rocket leaves or lamb's lettuce

Take a screw-topped jam jar and fill with the dressing ingredients. Replace the lid firmly and shake well until mixed. Pour into a large salad bowl. Add the spring onions, celery and fennel and toss well to coat the vegetables.

To prepare the rest of the salad, break the lettuces into manageable pieces. Halve the cucumber lengthways, then cut across into fairly thick slices. Have the rocket or lamb's lettuce ready.

Gently lay half this mixture on the dressing. Sprinkle with a little salt and pepper before adding the remaining salad. Toss the salad just before serving.

PREPARE AHEAD
You can prepare the salad several hours in advance, say on the morning of a dinner party. Put the bowl with the dressing, spring onions, celery and fennel in the fridge, covered. Put the prepared salad leaves and cucumber in a large plastic bag in the fridge. When it is time to serve, simply empty the contents of the bag into the bowl, season and toss in the dressing.

Onion & Soured Cream Salad

Simple, delicious and unusual. Serve this salad with cold meats, and grilled or poached fish, such as Chilled Celebration Salmon (page 104).

SERVES 4–6
2 very large, mild Spanish onions, cut in 5mm (¼ in) slices
1 × 250g carton full-fat crème fraîche
2 tablespoons snipped fresh chives
½ teaspoon sugar
Salt and freshly ground black pepper

To garnish
Approx. 8 whole chive stems, and chive flowers if available

PREPARE AHEAD
The prepared salad can be kept covered in the fridge for up to 2 days.

Put the sliced onions in a bowl and cover generously with boiling water. Cover and leave aside for 30 minutes.

Drain the onions in a colander, then pat dry on kitchen paper. Mix the crème fraîche, chives and sugar, add the onions, then taste and season with salt and pepper.

Turn into a shallow, rectangular serving dish, cover with clingfilm, then chill until ready to serve. Lay the chive stems obliquely down the length of the dish, scatter with chive flowers and serve.

Spicy Mexican Bean Salad

This recipe is even better if prepared in advance (to the point where the Tabasco sauce is added), so that the flavours have time to develop. Try this spicy accompaniment with Butterflied Lamb in Lemon Marinade (page 76) or Sea Bass with Citrus Salsa (page 74).

SERVES 6 AS A SIDE SALAD

1 × 420g tin flageolet beans
2 garlic cloves
2.5cm (1in) fresh ginger root, peeled
3 tablespoons sunflower oil
1 large onion, finely chopped
1 teaspoon ground cumin
1 teaspoon ground coriander
½ teaspoon chilli powder
1 teaspoon salt
1 red pepper, deseeded and diced
2 celery sticks, diced
2 tablespoons tomato purée
Juice of 1 lemon
1 teaspoon sugar
A few drops of Tabasco sauce (optional)
Freshly ground black pepper

To garnish
2 tablespoons chopped fresh mint
2 tablespoons chopped fresh coriander

Drain the beans in a colander, then dry on kitchen paper and transfer to a large bowl. Chop the garlic and ginger together very finely.

Heat the oil in a medium-sized frying pan and fry the onion for about 5 minutes over a low to moderate heat. Stir in the garlic and ginger and continue cooking for a further 5 minutes or until the onion is softened and golden. Sprinkle in the cumin, coriander and chilli powder and continue to cook for 1–2 minutes, stirring.

Scrape the contents of the pan into the bowl containing the beans. Add the remaining ingredients, stir well, then taste and season carefully with pepper and extra salt if necessary. If you would prefer the salad more chilli-hot, add a few drops of Tabasco sauce.

Spoon the salad into a serving bowl. Sprinkle thickly with the chopped mint and coriander and loosely fork the herbs into the bean mixture. Serve at room temperature.

PREPARE AHEAD
Prepare the salad without the herbs, cover with clingfilm and chill for up to 2 days. Toss with the herbs before serving. Not suitable for freezing.

Scandinavian Cucumber Salad

A well-behaved salad that can wait around until you are ready to serve, this is also one of those basic salads that goes with just about everything and always has a place on a buffet table. One of my all-time favourites is cucumber salad served with hot or cold poached salmon or try this with the Danish-style Open Sandwiches on page 128.

SERVES 6–8 AS A SIDE SALAD

2 large cucumbers
1 tablespoons salt
black pepper
4 tablespoons caster sugar
4 tablespoons white wine vinegar
2 tablespoons snipped fresh chives
2 tablespoons chopped fresh dill

To garnish
A few sprigs of fresh dill

Top, tail and peel the cucumbers, then slice thinly into a bowl. Add the salt, pepper, sugar and vinegar, then use your hands to turn the cucumber slices evenly in the mixture. Cover and chill for a minimum of 1 hour.

Turn the contents of the bowl into a colander and leave for about 10 minutes to drain thoroughly. Sprinkle with the chives and dill and turn the slices again with your hands to mix then check the seasoning. Transfer the cucumber to a serving dish and garnish with extra sprigs of dill.

PREPARE AHEAD
The salad can be prepared without the herbs, covered and kept in the fridge for up to 24 hours. Add the herbs just before serving.

Chorizo, Avocado & Tomato Salad with a Warm Dressing

This is delicious served at lunch with crusty bread. Or scale up the quantities and try with Red Pepper & Fennel Pissaladière (page 100).

SERVES 6

5 tablespoons olive oil
4 thick slices of white bread,
    crusts removed and cut
    into 2cm cubes
2 × 130g packets thinly sliced chorizo
3 large Little Gem lettuces
1 large ripe avocado, sliced into pieces
250g (9oz) cherry tomatoes, halved
1 small bunch of basil, roughly chopped
Salt and freshly ground black pepper
2 tablespoons balsamic vinegar
½ teaspoon caster sugar

Heat 2 tablespoons of oil in a frying pan, add the cubes of bread and fry until golden and crispy to make croutons. Using a slotted spoon, transfer to some kitchen paper and sprinkle with salt and pepper.

Add the chorizo to the pan, fry until crisp and golden (you may need to do this in batches).

Slice the lettuce and arrange in a salad bowl or on a platter. Add the avocado, cherry tomatoes, basil, croutons, fried chorizo and season with a little salt and pepper.

Add the balsamic vinegar, sugar and remaining oil to the pan, mix to incorporate the flavours in the pan then pour over the salad. Toss and serve.

PREPARE AHEAD
The salad can be assembled, without the avocado and dressing, up to 6 hours ahead. Slice the avocado at the last minute and add to the salad along with the warm dressing.

SOMETHING SWEET

*

Delicious desserts, comforting
puddings & puddings for crowds

T HERE ARE TWO very different types of sweet in this
chapter: cold and hot, or summery treats and winter
comfort food. Many of the puddings here can be eaten
warm or cold, but I personally think they taste best warm.

You can vary the fruit depending on what's in season (Bramley
Caramel on page 180 works well with apricots or rhubarb instead
of apples). There are different flavours after the Red Plum Ice
Cream to try (page 158). And most usefully, many of the recipes
in this chapter can be prepared in advance, at least a day ahead,
making them great for entertaining.

Some puddings are a little complicated but there are plenty
of easy recipes to balance them out. I've tried to use shortcuts
or find easier techniques to achieve the same end to save time.
Banoffee Brandy Snap Baskets (page 166) are a good example
of a tricky recipe made simple – this recipe is a total cheat but
a good dish to keep up your sleeve.

I'm not adverse to some ready-made help every so often, but
generally all the recipes can be made from scratch without
too much bother – my Velvet Chocolate Torte (page 194) is
a good example of straightforward recipe that tastes and
looks absolutely gorgeous!

Raspberry Jelly with Yoghurt 'Brûlée' Topping

This is lovely for all the family. The sugar topping isn't really caramelized but simply looks like it is because the sugar melts while the desserts chill in the fridge. If you wish, add a dash of raspberry liqueur or vodka to the jelly in place of some of the cold water.

SERVES 6

1 × 135g packet raspberry jelly

250g (9oz) fresh or frozen raspberries

200ml (7fl oz) double cream,
    lightly whipped

200g (7oz) full-fat Greek yoghurt

50g (2oz) light muscovado sugar

PREPARE AHEAD
The jelly part can be made in the glasses up to 2 days ahead. Add the cream and sugar up to 2 hours ahead. Not suitable for freezing.

Snip the jelly into pieces into a jug. Pour over 150ml (¼ pint) boiling water and stir until dissolved. Add enough cold water to make up to 600ml (1 pint).

Divide the raspberries between six pretty glasses. Pour in the jelly and transfer to the fridge to set for a minimum of 4 hours.

Mix the cream and yoghurt together in a bowl. Spoon on top of the set jelly and sprinkle with the sugar. Return to the fridge for another hour until the sugar starts to melt – this is a soft sugar topping.

Serve chilled.

Red Plum Ice Cream

Start the recipe the day before you want to serve it. Taste the plum purée, once sieved, and if it's a little too sharp add a little more caster sugar. See also the following different flavoured ice creams to try.

SERVES 8

1 tablespoon water
175g (6oz) caster sugar
225g (8oz) red plums
A little lemon juice, to taste
4 eggs, separated
300ml (10fl oz) double cream

Measure the water and 50g (2oz) of the caster sugar into a pan. Add the plums and adjust the heat to give a very gentle simmer. Cover and cook until tender then cool.

Have a plastic sieve positioned over a bowl. Empty the contents of the pan into the bowl, then rub the fruit through the sieve. Discard any skin and stones left behind and add a little lemon juice (and a little more sugar, to taste). Cover and chill in the fridge.

Put the egg whites in a large, grease-free bowl, then, using an electric hand whisk, whisk the whites at full speed until like a cloud.

Gradually whisk in the remaining sugar, a teaspoon at a time. When all the sugar has been added the meringue should be stiff and form sharp, glossy peaks. Beat the egg yolks and fold in.

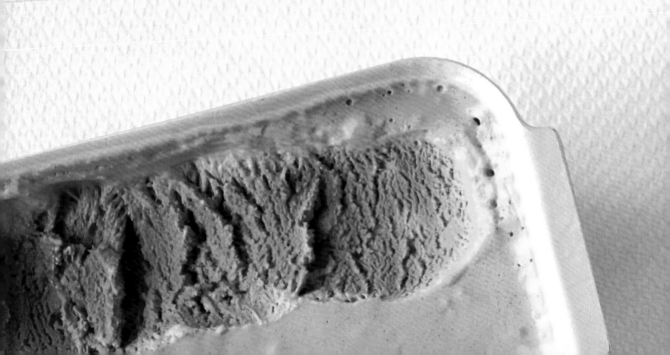

Quickly whisk the cream until thick and fold into the meringue mixture, followed by the plum purée. Pour the mixture into a shallow plastic freezer container and freeze overnight or for at least 12 hours. Transfer the container to the fridge about 20 minutes before scooping.

BLACKCURRANT ICE CREAM

Following the above recipe, use 75ml (3fl oz) sweetened blackcurrant purée or 6 tablespoons of blackcurrant squash in place of the plums. Whisk the egg whites with 100g (4oz) caster sugar, then fold in the egg yolks and squash. Pour into the container and swirl a seventh spoon of squash through the top of the ice cream to marble it. Freeze as directed in the recipe above.

LEMON & LIME ICE CREAM

Following the above recipe, use the strained juice of 1 large lemon and 1 large lime in place of the plums. Whisk the egg whites with 100g (4oz) caster sugar, then fold in the egg yolks and juices. Taste; you may prefer to add a little more sugar.

COFFEE ICE CREAM

Following the above recipe, add 4 tablespoons of liquid coffee essence (or 2 teaspoons of instant coffee dissolved in 2 tablespoons hot water) in place of the plums. Whisk the egg whites with 100g (4oz) caster sugar, then fold in the egg yolks and coffee.

Lemon & Lime Mousse

This is very light and healthy, with no cream added.

SERVES 6

1 × 11g packet powdered gelatine
4 eggs, separated
100g (4oz) caster sugar
Finely grated zest and juice of 2 limes
Finely grated zest and juice of 1 lemon

You will need a 1-litre (2-pint) glass dish or 8 glasses. Measure 4 tablespoons of cold water into a small bowl and sprinkle the powdered gelatine on top. Set aside until like sponge. Heat a pan of hot water and sit the bowl of gelatine inside until dissolved (do not stir). Leave to cool a little – it should still be runny.

Whisk the egg whites until stiff, using an electric hand whisk. In a separate bowl, whisk the egg yolks and sugar together until light, pale and thick so when the whisks are lifted out they leave an impression.

Add the cooled, dissolved gelatine to the egg yolk mixture, then add the zest and juice of the limes and lemon and stir carefully. Add 4 tablespoons of the whisked egg whites and mix in to loosen the mixture. Carefully fold in the remaining egg whites until smooth Spoon into the dish and chill for 8 hours. Serve chilled.

PREPARE AHEAD
Can be prepared up to 2 days ahead.

Mango Passion

Very easy to make, this dessert is better when made ahead as it allows the flavours of the mango and passion fruit to develop in the cream and yoghurt, and the dark sugar topping has time to liquify and sweeten each spoonful as you eat. Delicious – this is one of Lucy's favourite flavour combinations.

SERVES 6

1 large, ripe mango
3 ripe passion fruit
1 × 500g tub full-fat Greek yoghurt
150ml (5fl oz) double cream, lightly whipped
75g (3oz) light muscovado sugar

You will need six stemmed glasses or syllabub cups.

Slice the flesh from each side of the flat mango stone. Remove the peel and cut the flesh in cubes. Try to remove as much flesh as possible from around the stone, then peel and cube this too.

Using a teaspoon, scoop the seeds and flesh from the passion fruit into a bowl then mix with the yoghurt and cream.

Put an equal quantity of the mango in each glass then fill with the yoghurt mixture. Chill for up to 8 hours. An hour or so before serving, sprinkle with sugar and return to the fridge until ready to serve.

Indulgent Chocolate Ice Cream

Simple and delicious – no messing around or fancy flavours, just the best chocolate ice cream. This works best with a 39 per cent cocoa solids chocolate. If you use posh chocolate (e.g. 70 per cent cocoa solids), be careful not to overheat it during melting and you may need to add a little more sugar as the chocolate is more bitter. Simple, easy ice cream, which does not need churning or an ice cream mixer.

SERVES 6

200g dark chocolate (39 per cent
   cocoa solids), chopped
4 eggs
100g (4oz) caster sugar
300ml double cream, whipped

PREPARE AHEAD
Can be made up to 1 month
ahead and kept in the freezer.

AGA
Add the broken chocolate to a
bowl and sit on the back of the
Aga or in the simmering oven
until just melted.

Place the chopped chocolate in a bowl and sit over a pan of just hot water. Leave to melt, stirring occasionally, then set aside to cool a little.

Separate the eggs. Whisk the egg whites with an electric mixer until stiff like a cloud. Still whisking on maximum speed, gradually add the sugar a teaspoon at a time until stiff and glossy and all the sugar is incorporated.

Stir the melted chocolate into the whipped cream, then add the egg yolks. Stir to blend. Add a third of the egg white mixture to the chocolate cream and mix until combined. Carefully fold in the remaining egg whites until smooth and combined.

Spoon into a container and freeze for a minimum of 8 hours or ideally overnight. Remove from the fridge about 10 minutes before serving. There is no need to stir during the freezing process, just make and freeze.

Boozy White Chocolate & Orange Délice

This is a wonderful combination of chocolate and orange. If making it for children, you can omit the Irish whisky cream liqueur.

SERVES 6

100g (4oz) Belgian white chocolate
    (minimum 45 per cent cocoa solids),
    roughly chopped
150ml (¼ pint) double cream
3 tablespoons Irish whisky
    cream liqueur
8 oranges
100g (4oz) full-fat cream cheese
4 cubes of dark chocolate
    (39 per cent cocoa solids), chopped

PREPARE AHEAD
Can be prepared up to a day
ahead and kept in the fridge.

Put the chopped white chocolate in a bowl, along with the cream and Irish whisky cream liqueur and sit over a pan of just hot water. Leave to melt, stirring occasionally, then set aside to cool a little.

Finely grate the zest of seven oranges and add to a large bowl. Remove the zest with a zester (you want thin strips) from the remaining orange and set aside to garnish. Add the cream cheese to the bowl and stir. Gradually pour in the white chocolate, slowly at first and whisking until smooth.

Cut the skins from all the oranges and cut the fruit into segments, cutting either side of the membrane. Then cut each segment into three. Squeeze the juice from the orange shells and add 2 tablespoons to the white chocolate mixture.

Take six wine glasses and divide the orange segments between the bases. Spoon the white chocolate mixture on top and sprinkle with the reserved zested orange zest. Chill for an hour before serving.

Chilled Blackberry Cheesecake

Here's a cheesecake recipe that's perfect for using up blackberries in season or ones you have frozen over the summer.

SERVES 6

3 teaspoons powdered gelatine
100g (4oz) ginger biscuits, crushed
50g (2oz) butter, melted
500g (1lb 2oz) fresh or frozen blackberries
100g (4oz) caster sugar
300g (10oz) full-fat cream cheese
200ml double cream, lightly whipped
A few fresh blackberries, for decoration

PREPARE AHEAD
The cheesecake can be made up to a day ahead and store, covered, in the fridge.

FREEZE
It freezes well, cooked and undecorated.

Line the base of a 20cm (8in) round springform tin with a circle of baking parchment.

Measure 4 tablespoons of cold water into a small bowl and sprinkle the powdered gelatine on top. Set aside until like sponge.

Mix the crushed biscuits and melted butter together in a bowl and stir to combine. Spoon into the tin and press down evenly using the back of a spoon.

Measure the fresh or frozen blackberries and half the sugar into a saucepan. Heat over a low heat, stirring until the blackberries have just softened. Press through a sieve and set aside to cool.

Heat a pan of hot water and sit the bowl of gelatine inside until dissolved (do not stir). Stir into the blackberry purée.

Measure the cream cheese and remaining sugar into a bowl and stir to combine. Slowly add the blackberry purée, stir to combine, then fold in the whipped cream. Mix until smooth and combined then pour into the tin and level the top.

Chill for 2–3 hours or until set. Use a small palette knife to loosen the cheesecake around the edges and remove from the tin. Decorate with a few fresh blackberries and cut into wedges to serve.

Banoffee Brandy Snap Baskets

This is a dessert that can be ready to go up to a week ahead of time. Don't be frightened away by the brandy snap baskets in the title because these are an enormous cheat. You buy the brandy snaps, soften them for a moment in the oven then mould them, so within 5 minutes of opening the packet, the little baskets are ready to use! The toffee sauce is brilliant with ice cream too.

SERVES 8
8 shop-bought brandy snaps
1–2 bananas
A little lemon juice
Vanilla ice cream

For the toffee sauce
50g (2oz) butter
150g (5oz) soft brown sugar
150g (5oz) golden syrup
1 × 170g tin evaporated milk

PREPARE AHEAD
The brandy snap baskets can be formed and stored in an airtight container for up to 2 weeks. The toffee sauce can be made and stored in a sealed container in the fridge for up to 3 weeks. If tossed in lemon juice the bananas can be kept for up to 3 hours at room temperature before draining and using.

Preheat the oven to 180°C/160°C fan/Gas 4. Line two baking trays with baking parchment. Have ready four spice jars or upturned teacups.

Arrange four brandy snaps on each of the two lined baking trays, then put one tray into the oven for about 1 minute. This is all the time the brandy snaps need to soften and unfold. Carefully lift the soft brandy snaps with a palette knife from the tray and lay them over the jars or cups. As soon as they are cool enough, mould each one into a ruffle-edged basket. Leave until cool and set before proceeding with the second batch.

To make the sauce, put the butter, sugar and syrup in a pan and heat gently until melted and liquid. Turn up the heat so the mixture boils gently for 5 minutes. Remove the pan from the heat and gradually stir in the evaporated milk. The sauce is now ready and can be served hot, warm or cold.

Just before serving, assemble the dessert. Slice the bananas then, if there is to be any delay, toss them in a little lemon juice to prevent them browning and drain before using. Arrange about three slices in the base of each basket, spoon in the ice cream then spoon over the toffee sauce. Serve immediately.

AGA
Soften the brandy snaps in the simmering oven until flattened. This will take 1–5 minutes, depending on the heat of the Aga.

Red Fruit Salad with Cassis

A fruit salad that can be served hot or chilled. I love to serve it warm because of the intoxicating aromas of all the different fruits that come wafting up from the plate. This very deep, dark red salad looks very pretty if served in a glass bowl on a plate lined with fresh blackcurrant or raspberry leaves. It is very simple to make and is a good way to use frozen currants.

SERVES 6–8

450g (1lb) redcurrants,
    stalks removed
450g (1lb) blackcurrants,
    stalks removed
75g (3oz) caster sugar
4 ripe nectarines, sliced
225g (8oz) fresh strawberries,
    halved if large
150g (5oz) fresh blueberries
450g (1lb) fresh raspberries
3 tablespoons crème de cassis liqueur

Put the redcurrants and blackcurrants in a pan with the sugar and warm gently, covered. As they begin to cook, the berries will release some of their juice and dissolve the sugar so no additional water is needed.

When the fruits are warm, remove the pan from the heat and add the nectarines, strawberries and blueberries. If you are intending to serve the salad warm, add the raspberries and cassis now. If the salad is to be served cold, pour the fruits into a serving dish and cool before putting in the fridge to chill. Just before serving, gently stir in the raspberries and cassis.

PREPARE AHEAD
The salad can be made without the raspberries and kept covered in the fridge for up to 24 hours. Reheat and add the raspberries just before serving.

FREEZE
Freeze for up to 3 months.

Almond Florentine Dessert

If ginger is not to your taste, sandwich with fresh raspberries and whipping cream. It is essential to measure or weigh the ingredients for the florentines carefully since even a minor variation can make a considerable difference. You must use good, solid baking trays that will not bend in the oven.

SERVES 8

For the almond florentines
150g (5oz) butter
120g (4½oz) caster sugar
1½ tablespoons plain flour
3 tablespoons milk
165g (5½oz) flaked almonds

For the filling
2 × 400g tins pear halves in juice
300ml (10fl oz) whipping cream
3 pieces stem ginger, finely chopped
2 tablespoons ginger syrup
2 tablespoons Poire Williams (pear) liqueur

To decorate
A little icing sugar, sifted

PREPARE AHEAD
The made pudding will keep for 24 hours. The filling can be made, covered and stored for up to 2 days in the fridge.

FREEZE
The almond florentines can be baked, cooled, left on their baking papers and stacked. Seal them inside a plastic bag, then store for up to 1 month. The florentines can be used straight from the freezer.

Preheat the oven to 180°C/160°C fan/Gas 4. Cut out three 25cm (10in) circles from baking parchment and place on three baking trays.

Gently melt the butter and sugar in a pan. Combine the flour and milk in a bowl and stir to form a paste. When the butter has melted, stir in the paste, followed by the almonds.

Bring to the boil and boil for 30 seconds. Divide the mixture equally between the trays and spread out very thinly to the edges of the circles. Bake, in rotation if necessary, for 9–11 minutes until a toffee-golden all over. Until you get the timing just right for your oven, watch carefully as the mixture can over-brown very quickly.

Remove from the oven. If the mixture has flowed a little outside the marked circles simply bring it back into line with a small palette knife, then leave to cool and set.

Drain the pears and discard the juice. Dry them well on kitchen paper, then coarsely chop. Pour the cream into a bowl and whisk until stiff enough to hold a shape. Fold in the pears, ginger, ginger syrup and liqueur.

Select the best almond florentine round for the top and reserve. Carefully, strip the baking parchment off the other two rounds and put one of them on a serving plate. Spread with half the filling and place the second round on top. Spread with the remaining filling then place the last and best florentine on top. Ideally, chill for 4 hours before serving – this is the perfect time to cut through the florentine.

AGA
Bake in the roasting oven a tray at a time on the grid shelf on the floor with the cold plain shelf on the second set of runners above for 7 minutes. Watch carefully during the last minutes of cooking.

Chilled Marbled Chocolate Cheesecake

We use a dark chocolate with 39 per cent cocoa solids because we find it melts perfectly and is not too bitter. If you are using a posh chocolate (70 per cent cocoa solids), be very careful not to overheat it when melting otherwise it will be lumpy. White chocolate can be tricky to melt, so heat it up very, very gently; otherwise it will split and not allow the cheesecake to set.

SERVES 6

For the base
100g (4oz) dark chocolate
    digestive biscuits, crushed
50g (2oz) butter, melted

For the filling
200g (7oz) Belgian white
    chocolate, chopped
300ml (½ pint) double cream
300g (10oz) full-fat cream cheese
½ teaspoon vanilla extract
100g (4oz) dark chocolate
    (39 per cent cocoa solids)

TO PREPARE AHEAD
Can be made up to 2 days
ahead and kept in the fridge.

TO FREEZE
Once set and chilled this
freezes well.

Line the base of a 20cm (8in) round, deep springform tin with a circle of baking parchment.

To make the base, mix the crushed biscuits with the melted butter and press into the base of the tin. Level using the back of a spoon.

To make the filling, put the chopped white chocolate in to a bowl and sit over a pan of just hot water. Leave to melt (but don't allow it to get too hot), stirring occasionally, then set aside to cool a little.

Reserve 3 tablespoons of the double cream. Pour the remainder into a large bowl, then add the cream cheese and vanilla. Whisk, using an electric hand whisk, until smooth. Add the melted white chocolate and whisk again until smooth and thick.

Spoon about 6 tablespoons of the white chocolate filling into a mixing bowl. Spoon the remaining mixture into the tin and smooth over the top. Chill for 30 minutes.

Add the reserved double cream to the reserved white chocolate mixture and mix together until smooth. Spoon over the set mixture in the tin.

Melt the dark chocolate as before and then drizzle over the top of the cheesecake and use the blade of a knife to swirl the toppings together.

Chill for a minimum of 2 hours, then turn out and cut into wedges to serve.

Chocolate & Orange Pavlova

This is a luxury pavlova of light, crisp meringue filled with a rich chocolate and orange mixture.

SERVES 8–10

For the meringue
3 egg whites
175g (6oz) caster sugar
1 teaspoon white wine vinegar
1 teaspoon cornflour

For the filling
100g (4oz) dark chocolate
   (39 per cent cocoa solids),
   broken into pieces
50g (2oz) caster sugar
3 tablespoons water
3 egg yolks
Grated zest of 1 small orange
1 tablespoon orange juice
300ml (10fl oz) double cream,
   chilled

To decorate
150ml (5fl oz) whipping cream
A little melted dark chocolate
   to decorate

Preheat the oven to 160°C/140°C fan/Gas 3. Cut out a 23cm (9in) circle from a piece of baking parchment and place on a baking tray.

Put the egg whites in a large, grease-free bowl and whisk on maximum speed using an electric hand whisk until stiff but not dry.

Gradually add the sugar a teaspoon at a time, whisking at full speed between each addition. When about two-thirds of the sugar has been added, the process can be speeded up; in total it should take about 8 minutes (2–3 minutes with one of the newest mixers).

Mix the vinegar and cornflour in a small bowl, then fold into the meringue. Spread the mixture on to the disc of baking parchment, making the meringue slightly hollow in the centre and higher around the sides. Transfer to the oven and immediately lower the temperature to 150°C/130°C fan/Gas 2.

Bake for 1 hour or until the meringue is firm to touch and a pale biscuit colour. Turn off the oven and leave the meringue inside the oven, for a further 1 hour. Set aside to cool. Carefully peel the baking parchment away from the base, then place the meringue on a serving dish. Cover and leave aside while making the filling.

Add the chocolate to a processor and whizz for 1 minute or until powdery. Alternatively, you can finely grate the chocolate.

Combine the sugar and water in a small pan and heat gently until the sugar has dissolved, stirring occasionally. Now turn up the heat and boil briskly for 3–4 minutes to obtain a thin syrup.

Set the processor containing the chocolate running and pour in the hot syrup through the funnel so that the chocolate melts and becomes liquid. Next, add the egg yolks, process for a few seconds, then add the orange zest and juice. If you are not using a processor, beat the ingredients together with a wooden spoon.

In a separate bowl, beat the cream to a soft, floppy consistency, then fold in the chocolate mixture. Pile the filling into the meringue then transfer to the fridge to chill for 2 hours.

Just before serving, whip the cream until stiff enough to pipe. Fill a piping bag fitted with a 6- or 8-point star nozzle and pipe swirls around the edge. Drizzle melted chocolate over the top to give a zigzag finish.

Chocolate Obsession

A gateau for a special occasion: four layers of cake with truffle filling and silky chocolate icing.

SERVES 10–12

For the sponge
350g (12oz) dark chocolate
   (39 per cent cocoa solids),
   broken into pieces
225g (8oz) butter, softened
3 eggs
400g (14oz) caster sugar
400g (14oz) self-raising flour
1½ teaspoons baking powder

For the truffle filling
225g (8oz) dark chocolate
   (39 per cent cocoa solids),
   broken into pieces
150ml double cream
150g (5oz) butter, softened
500g (1lb 2oz) icing sugar, sifted

For the ganache icing
225g (8oz) dark chocolate
   (39 per cent cocoa solids),
   broken into pieces
125ml (4½fl oz) double cream

Preheat the oven 160C/140Fan/Gas 3. You will need 2 × deep 23cm (9inch) round loose-bottomed or springform tin, greased and base lined.

To make the cake, put the broken pieces of chocolate and butter into a pan. Add 300ml water and heat gently over a low heat, stirring until melted and smooth. Cool slightly.

Break the eggs into a mixing bowl and beat with a fork. Add the caster sugar and beat again until smooth. Gradually pour in the melted chocolate mixture and whisk by hand until smooth. Sift the flour and baking powder into the chocolate mixture and mix until smooth.

Divide evenly between the cake tins. Bake for 1–1¼ hours or until springy to the touch and shrinking away from the edges of the tin. After 10 minutes turn on to a wire rack to cool and remove the paper.

To make the filling, sit a bowl over a pan of simmering water. Add the chocolate and cream to the bowl and gently melt, stirring until smooth.

Remove from the heat, add the butter to the hot chocolate and cream and stir until smooth. Sift in half the icing sugar, and mix, then add the remaining icing sugar and mix until smooth. Set aside to cool until thick.

To make the ganache icing, gently heat the cream in a pan. Add the broken chocolate to the hot cream and stir until melted.

PREPARE AHEAD
The cake can be made and
assembled the day ahead and
kept in the fridge – best to ice
with the ganache icing on the
day of serving.

FREEZE
Cakes freeze well filled but
not iced.

AGA
Bake on grid shelf on the floor
of the roasting oven, with the
cold sheet on the second set of
runners for about 35 minutes.
Transfer the hot cold sheet to
the simmering oven and sit
the cake on top and bake for
a further 35 minutes, or until
cooked right through.

Slice each cake in half horizontally and sit one piece on a plate. Divide the truffle filling into three and spread a third of the filling on top of one cake, repeat so you have four layers of cake and three layers of filling. The side of the cake needs to be exactly level, if not trim with a serrated knife. Pour the ganache icing over the top of the cake and let it run down the sides, using a palette knife to spread it evenly over the top and the sides of the cake to give a smooth shiny glaze.

Set aside until firm then cut into wedges to serve.

Toffee Apple Steamed Pudding

This recipe is for a pudding made in a large basin but the mixture will also fill six timbale moulds or ramekins, baked for 35 minutes.

SERVES 6–8

For the toffee sauce
200g (7oz) butter
200g (7oz) light muscovado sugar
Juice of ½ a lemon
2 dessert apples, peeled,
    cored and cut into tiny pieces

For the sponge
100g (4oz) butter, softened
50g (2oz) light muscovado sugar
1 tablespoon golden syrup
2 eggs
150g (5oz) self-raising flour
1 teaspoon baking powder

PREPARE AHEAD
The pudding can be made and kept in the basin up to 6 hours ahead.

FREEZE
It freezes well once cooked, for up to 3 months.

AGA
Bring to the boil on the boiling plate, cover and transfer to the simmering oven for 2 hours.

Grease a 1-litre (2-pint) pudding basin.

To make the toffee sauce, melt the butter and sugar together in a saucepan until the sugar is melted and combined. Add the lemon juice and remove from the heat.

Pour half of the mixture into the pudding basin – reserve the remaining sauce to serve separately. Add the chopped apple to the basin.

Measure the cake ingredients into a bowl and whisk together until just blended. Spoon into the basin.

Take a square of foil a little bigger than the top of the basin, fold a pleat down the centre and grease the underside. Sit on top of the bowl, seal around the edges or tie with string to hold in place.

Place a metal cookie cutter or enamel side plate in the base of a deep saucepan and sit the basin on top. Fill up halfway with boiling water, cover and bring to the boil on the hob. Once boiling, lower the temperature and simmer for 1½ hours until well risen and firm to the touch.

Remove the foil, place the pudding on to a lipped dish or plate and remove the basin. Cut into wedges and serve with the remaining warm toffee sauce.

Melting Chocolate Fondants

Such a popular dessert – the chocolate puddings should be runny in the centre once baked so be careful not to overcook them. Serve with ice cream.

MAKES 8

200g (7oz) dark chocolate
    (39 per cent cocoa solids), chopped
200g (7oz) butter, cubed
150g (5oz) caster sugar
5 eggs
50g (2oz) cocoa powder

For the chocolate sauce
150g (5oz) dark chocolate
    (39 per cent cocoa solids)
200ml double cream

PREPARE AHEAD
Can be made up to a day ahead and kept in the fridge, uncooked in the moulds. You can make the sauce up to 2 days ahead, keep it in the fridge and gently reheat to serve.

FREEZE
The puddings freeze well in their moulds, uncooked. The sauce can't be frozen.

AGA
Bake the fondants on the second set of runners in the roasting oven for about 8 minutes. For the sauce, sit a bowl of the chopped chocolate and cream on the back of the Aga until melted.

Preheat the oven to 200°C/180°C fan/Gas 6. You will need 8 metal dariole moulds, or ramekins, greased with butter.

Add the chopped chocolate to a bowl, along with the butter and sit over a pan of just hot water. Leave to melt, stirring occasionally, then set aside to cool a little.

Measure the caster sugar and eggs into a bowl and whisk using an electric hand whisk until pale, light and thick and the mixture leaves an impression when the whisks are lifted out.

Fold the melted chocolate into the egg mixture, sieve in the cocoa powder and carefully cut and fold until smooth – be careful not to beat otherwise it will lose its air. Spoon into the prepared moulds.

Sit on a baking sheet and bake for 8–10 minutes until well risen and firm around the edges.

To make the sauce, break the chocolate into a bowl, add the cream, and sit over a pan of simmering water until the chocolate has melted. Stir until smooth.

Run a palette knife around the chocolate puddings and tip out of the moulds on to plates. Pour over the sauce and serve.

Bramley Caramel

This is a very adaptable recipe. You can use dessert or cooking apples, whichever you have to hand, or rhubarb works well. Adding about nine halved, easy-cook apricots to the apples is also a favourite of mine.

SERVES 6–8

175g (6oz) self-raising flour

1 teaspoon baking powder

50g (2oz) caster sugar

50g (2oz) softened butter

1 egg

Grated zest of 1 lemon

150ml (5fl oz) milk

A generous 450g (1lb) apples, peeled and cut into 5mm (¼-in) slices

50g (2oz) butter, melted

Approx. 175g (6oz) demerara sugar

To serve
Crème fraîche

TIP
If you are making caramel for something like crème caramel, do not attempt this in a pan that is non-stick or has a dark interior. You cannot see clearly when the caramel is dark enough, and I have found it impossible to make caramel in a non-stick saucepan as the syrup crystallizes and will not caramelize. Heavy-gauge aluminium or stainless-steel pans are better for this.

Preheat the oven to 200°C/180°C fan/Gas 6. Grease well a shallow, ovenproof baking dish about 28cm (11in) in diameter.

Measure the flour, baking powder, caster sugar, butter, egg, lemon zest and milk into a bowl. Beat together until the mixture forms a soft, cake-like consistency. Spread this mixture in the base of the prepared dish and arrange the apple slices on top.

Brush or drizzle the butter over the apple, then sprinkle with the demerara sugar. Bake for about 35 minutes or until the top has caramelized to a deep golden brown. Serve warm with the crème fraîche.

PREPARE AHEAD
Have the sponge made and spread in the dish. Cover with clingfilm and keep in the fridge for up to 8 hours. Prepare the apples and finish the topping while the oven is heating.

FREEZE
Freezes well cooked, for up to 3 months.

AGA
Place on the grid shelf on the floor of the roasting oven and bake for about 25 minutes until the apples are pale golden and the sponge is cooked. If the top is getting too brown before the sponge is cooked, slide the cold plain shelf above on the second set of runners.

Classic Apple Cinnamon Crumble

*A classic crumble topping –
no fancy oats or cereals, just
full of flavour and perfect
for a comforting pudding.
Serve with custard, cream
or ice cream.*

SERVES 6
25g (1oz) butter
1kg (2¼lb) cooking apples, peeled,
    cored and thickly sliced
75g (3oz) sultanas
1 teaspoon ground cinnamon
100g (4oz) demerara sugar

For the topping
175g (6oz) plain flour
75g (3oz) butter, cubed
50g (2oz) demerara sugar
25g (1oz) flaked almonds

Preheat the oven to 200°C/180°C fan/Gas 6.
You will need a shallow 1.5-litre (2½ pint)
ovenproof dish.

Melt the butter in a saucepan. Add the apples,
sultanas, cinnamon and sugar and stir over a
high heat for 2–3 minutes until the sugar has
melted. Spoon into the dish.

To make the crumble topping, measure
the flour, butter and sugar into a bowl. Rub
together using your fingers until it looks
like breadcrumbs. Sprinkle on top of the
apples in the dish and scatter with the
flaked almonds.

Bake for 35–40 minutes or until lightly
golden brown and bubbling.

PREPARE AHEAD
The crumble can be assembled
up to 6 hours ahead.

FREEZE
It freezes well uncooked in
the dish for up to 3 months.

AGA
Bake on the second set of
runners in the roasting oven
for about 35 minutes.

Apricot & Almond Torte

Perfect for a Sunday lunch, this is a very thin, golden dessert served with crème fraîche or pouring cream.

SERVES 8

75g (3oz) butter, softened

75g (3oz) caster sugar

75g (3oz) self-raising flour

25g (1oz) ground almonds

1 teaspoon baking powder

1 teaspoon almond extract

2 eggs

2 × 400g tins apricot halves in juice

3 tablespoons apricot jam

50g (2oz) toasted flaked almonds

PREPARE AHEAD
The torte is best made and served immediately, but if you have some left over it reheats well the next day.

AGA
Bake on the grid shelf of the floor of the roasting oven for 20–25 minutes. If getting too brown, slide a cold sheet on to the second set of runners.

Preheat the oven to 200°C/180°C Fan/Gas 6. Grease a 28cm (11in) fluted loose-bottomed tin with butter.

Measure the butter, sugar, flour, ground almonds, baking powder, almond extract and eggs into a bowl. Beat together until smooth. Spread out over the base of the greased tin.

Drain the apricots and dry with kitchen paper. Arrange, cut-side down, over the surface of the mixture. Bake for about 20–25 minutes, until the sponge is lightly golden brown and well risen.

Melt the jam in a saucepan over a low heat until just melted. Brush over the sponge and apricots and scatter with the flaked almonds. Remove the torte from the tin while warm and serve cut into wedges.

Granny's Plum Pie

I often make this for my grandchildren, and it's perfect for using up windfall plums. When making rough puff pastry, it is important that the butter and lard are stone cold as they have to be grated.

SERVES 6–8

For the rough puff pastry
225g (8oz) plain flour
100g (4oz) butter, chilled
50g (2oz) lard, chilled

For the filling
1.5kg (3lb) just-ripe plums
175g (6oz) caster sugar
2 level tablespoons cornflour

To glaze
1 egg, beaten

PREPARE AHEAD
The pie can be assembled
up to 6 hours ahead.

FREEZE
It freezes well uncooked.

AGA
Bake on the lowest set of
runners in the roasting oven
with the cold sheet on the
second set of runners for
50 minutes.

Preheat the oven to 200°C/180°C fan/Gas 6. You will need a 2-litre (3½-pint) pie dish. To make the pastry, measure the flour into a mixing bowl. Using a coarse grater, grate half the butter into the bowl. Using your fingers, flick over some of the flour to cover the butter. Grate in the remaining butter, coat with more flour, then grate in the lard. Using your fingers, coat the fat with flour. Add enough water to bring together and then knead to form a ball.

Roll out the pastry on a floured work surface to about 12cm × 30cm. Fold the top half of the pastry into the middle and the bottom half over the top. Turn the pastry 45 degrees so it looks like a book. Reroll out and fold as before. Rest in the fridge for 15 minutes. Repeat this process two more times until the pastry has a total of four rolls and folds.

Slice each plum in half and remove the stone, then tip into a bowl. Mix the sugar and the cornflour together, then add to the plums and toss together. Spoon into the dish and place a pie funnel in the middle.

Roll out the pastry slightly larger than the top of the dish. Wet the lip of the dish and cut strips of pastry to lay all around the lip. Wet these and place the large piece of pastry on top, pushing down to seal the edges and making sure the pie funnel is poking through the middle of the pastry. Knock up the edges using the back of a knife. Brush the top of the pastry with beaten egg.

Bake for 55 minutes to 1 hour, until golden and crisp.

Pear & Lemon Curd Tart

This tart, as with French pastries, works so well with under-ripe fruit. If your pears are ripe, just cook them in the syrup for a little less time (5–10 minutes).

SERVES 8

For the pastry
300g (10oz) plain flour
150g (5oz) icing sugar
150g (5oz) butter, cubed
1 egg

For the filling
100g (4oz) caster sugar
6 pears, preferably under-ripe
200g (7oz) full-fat cream cheese
450g (1lb) good-quality lemon curd
Finely grated zest of 1 lemon
1 egg

PREPARE AHEAD
The tart can be made and cooked up to 8 hours ahead – reheat gently in a very low oven.

AGA
Bake on the floor of the roasting oven for about 35–40 minutes. If the tart gets too brown, slide the cold sheet on the second set of runners.

Preheat the oven to 200°C/180°C fan/Gas 6 and put a baking sheet in to get hot. You will need a 28cm (11in) deep, fluted, loose-bottomed flan tin.

To make the pastry, measure the flour, icing sugar and butter into a processor and whizz until it looks like breadcrumbs. Add the egg and whizz again until it forms a dough. Tip on to a floured worktop and knead lightly. Remove a little less than half the pastry, wrap in clingfilm and chill in the fridge. Roll the remaining pastry a little bigger than the tin and use to line the base and sides, forming a lip around the edge of the tin. Chill in the fridge.

To make the filling, measure the sugar into a shallow, wide-based saucepan, add 300ml water and stir over a gentle heat until the sugar has dissolved. Remove from the heat.

Peel the pears, slice in half through the stem and remove the core. Add the pears to the sugar syrup in the pan. Bring to the boil, cover, lower the heat and gently simmer for 12–15 minutes until just tender. Drain and leave to cool.

Measure the cream cheese, lemon curd, lemon zest and egg into a bowl and whisk until smooth.

Prick the base of the pastry with a fork. Spread the lemon filling over the pastry base and arrange the pears, cut-side down, on top. Roll out the reserved pastry, large enough to cover the top. Lift the pastry over the top and seal the edges by pressing the pastry edges together.

Sit the tart on the hot baking sheet in the oven and bake for 40–45 minutes or until the pastry is cooked and lightly golden. Leave to cool for 10 minutes before cutting into wedges.

Marmalade Bread & Butter Pudding

A great family favourite as a pudding to follow a weekend lunch. Ideally, use a rectangular dish simply because the bread fits it better. If you are not keen on sultanas, just leave them out.

SERVES 6–8

100g (4oz) butter, melted

8 thin slices of white bread

4 tablespoons marmalade

75g (3oz) sugar

100g (4oz) sultanas

2 eggs

300ml (½ pint) double cream

150 ml (¼ pint) milk

Finely grated zest of 1 orange

PREPARE AHEAD
You can keep the prepared pudding (but without the custard poured over) covered in the fridge for up to 6 hours. Pour the custard over about 1 hour before baking.

AGA
Bake on the grid shelf on the floor of the roasting oven. Cook for about 20–25 minutes or until golden brown and crisp.

Preheat the oven to 180°C/160°C fan/Gas 4. Use a little of the melted butter to grease a 1.5-litre (2½-pint) ovenproof dish measuring about 18 × 23 × 5cm (7 × 9 × 2in).

Use the melted butter to butter one side of each slice of bread. Spread the marmalade on to four slices and sandwich together to make four marmalade sandwiches.

Slice the crusts from the sandwiches and cut each into four triangles. Put four triangles into the base of the dish and sprinkle over half of the sugar and sultanas. Arrange the remaining sandwiches in lines on top, then sprinkle over the remaining sugar and fruit.

Beat together the eggs, cream and milk and orange zest in a bowl and pour over the pudding. Leave to stand for about 1 hour if time allows.

Bake for about 40 minutes or until the top is golden brown and crisp and the pudding slightly puffed up. Serve hot – though there are some who insist that it is delicious cold!

Gratin of Exotic Fruits

This is a store-cupboard fall-back recipe that relies on three tins and one or two cartons. If it really is an emergency, you might not have time to chill the pudding sufficiently. Don't worry, push it into the freezer to speed things up; it will only need about 30 minutes. Then the sugar can go on and the pudding can be grilled. Just make sure you put the fruit into the sort of dish that can stand the change in temperature!

SERVES 6
1 × 400g tin mango slices
1 × 400g tin mandarin slices
1 × 400g tin lychees
600ml (1 pint) double cream
100g (4oz) light muscovado sugar

PREPARE AHEAD
Have the pudding ready, topped with cream but not sugar, and keep covered in the fridge for up to 48 hours. Add the sugar just before grilling, then follow the recipe above.

AGA
Slide the pudding on to the top set of runners in the roasting oven for 5 minutes, or until the sugar has caramelized.

Empty the tins of fruit into a colander and drain thoroughly, then tip out on to several sheets of kitchen paper to mop up any remaining moisture. Arrange the fruit to cover the base of a shallow, flameproof dish and gently press the fruits down to even them out and level the surface.

Lightly whip the cream until it is floppy, then spread over the fruits to the edge of the dish. Chill for at least 2 hours; the cream needs to be very cold and firm. Leave the dish in the fridge right up to the last moment. If short of time, put the cream-topped pudding in the freezer for about 30 minutes or until the cream is firm.

Preheat the grill to maximum. Spread the sugar evenly over the cream and grill for about 1–2 minutes, or until the sugar becomes liquid and darkens. Watch the pudding constantly as it caramelizes – the process happens so rapidly it can blacken and easily burn unless you are careful. Give the caramel 1–2 minutes to cool and become brittle, then serve.

Mini Banoffee Pies

Everyone's favourite dessert – these individual pies are Lucy's recipe and are divine. Tins of ready-made caramel can be bought in any supermarket and save having to boil a can of condensed milk like we used to, to give it a caramel flavour.

SERVES 8

For the base
40g (1½oz) butter, melted
75g (3oz) digestive biscuits, crushed

For the topping
50g (2oz) butter
50g (2oz) light muscovado sugar
1 × 397g tin caramel
4 small bananas
200ml (7fl oz) double cream,
    lightly whipped
25g (1oz) square of dark chocolate

PREPARE AHEAD
The toffee can be put into the rings up to a day ahead. Top with banana and cream up to 6 hours ahead (leave the rings on as the banana will discolour if exposed to the air). Not suitable for freezing.

You will need eight 7cm (2½-in) cooking rings, arranged on a baking sheet.

To make the bases, mix the melted butter with the crushed biscuits and stir until combined. Spoon evenly between the rings and press down with the back of a spoon. Chill while you make the topping.

Melt the butter in a saucepan then add the sugar and stir until dissolved. Add the caramel and stir until combined. Simmer for 1 minute then set aside to cool for a few minutes.

Pour the sauce into the rings on top of the biscuit base and chill for about 1 hour or until the toffee has just set. Slice the banana and arrange on top, then spoon or pipe over the cream.

Slide a fish slice under each ring and move to serving plates. Remove the rings and finely grate chocolate on top of each pie to garnish. Serve chilled.

Hazelnut Pavlova

*A classic pavlova with the addition
of chopped hazelnuts. Don't be
tempted to chop the nuts in the food
processor, because the texture is
best chopped by hand to give it
a crunchy bite.*

SERVES 6

3 egg whites

175g (6oz) caster sugar

1 teaspoon cornflour

1 teaspoon white wine vinegar

50g (2oz) toasted hazelnuts, chopped

350g (12oz) raspberries

300ml (½ pint) double cream,
  whipped

PREPARE AHEAD

The pavlova can be made up
to 1 month ahead and kept in
a dry cool place. Fill with
cream and raspberries about
4 hours before serving.

FREEZE

It freezes well unfilled,
carefully wrapped.

AGA

Bake in the simmering oven
for 1½ hours or longer, until
it easily comes off the paper.

Preheat the oven to 160°C/140°C fan/Gas 3.
Line a baking sheet with baking parchment.

Whisk the egg whites using an electric hand
whisk until stiff and like a cloud. Gradually,
still whisking on maximum speed, add the
sugar a teaspoon at a time until incorporated
and stiff and shiny.

Mix the cornflour with the vinegar in a cup
and stir into the meringue. Add the hazelnuts.

Spread the meringue on the baking sheet to
a 10 × 30cm (4 × 12in) rectangle, or a 25cm
(10in) circle if you prefer. Build up the sides
slightly so there is a well in the middle.

Transfer to the oven and immediately turn
the temperature down to 150°C/130°C fan/
Gas 2. Bake for 1 hour, then turn the oven
off and leave for another hour.

Set aside to cool and, when completely cold,
remove from the paper to a flat plate. Stir
half the raspberries into the whipped cream
and spoon into the middle of the pavlova.
Scatter the remaining raspberries on top.

Cut into slices or wedges to serve.

Quite the Best Fruit Salad

It's quite the best because it can be made ahead. This recipe includes sugar, but I very often leave it out when I serve this as an alternative alongside rich puddings. Ripe fruits are sweet enough without sugar, so better not to use it, if you can!

SERVES AT LEAST 10–12

For the basic fruit salad
1 charentais melon
1 galia or honeydew melon
100g (4oz) caster sugar
6 thin-skinned oranges
1 pink grapefruit
1 ripe pineapple
1 ripe mango

Later additions
225g (8oz) seedless red or green grapes
   or strawberries or raspberries

PREPARE AHEAD
The basic fruit salad can be kept covered in the fridge for up to 24 hours. Add the grapes or soft fruit just before serving.

You will need a very sharp knife and a large container that will store the fruit salad in the fridge.

To prepare the melons, halve, scoop out the seeds with a spoon, then cut each one into a total of 6–8 wedges. Remove the rind and cut the flesh into chunks. Transfer the prepared melon and any juices to the container and sprinkle with a little of the measured sugar.

Peel the oranges then slice the fruit into thin rounds, not segments. Prepare the grapefruit in the same manner, but this time cut into segments, removing any white membrane. Transfer the citrus fruit and any juices to the container and sprinkle with a little more of the sugar.

Top and tail the pineapple. Sit it on its cut base, then cut away a strip of rind, working from the top to the base of the fruit and following the shape. Work your way around the fruit in this fashion until all the rind has been removed. Quarter the fruit lengthways then trim away the central, woody core. Slice the strips of pineapple across into chunks. Add the fruit and juices to the container and sprinkle with the last of the sugar.

To prepare the mango, cut off thick slices above and below the flat stone, then peel off the skin. Cut the flesh into cubes. Add all the mango to the container.

Cover the fruit salad and chill for about 2 hours Just before serving, add the grapes, strawberries or raspberries. Transfer the fruit salad to a serving bowl and take it to the table.

Velvet Chocolate Torte

Yes, it really does serve 12, it is so rich! If you do not have a springform tin, spoon the mixture into a freezer-safe bowl, cover with clingfilm, then freeze. After thawing for 20 minutes the chocolate will be ready to spoon on to serving plates and be decorated with strawberries. You can make half the quantity if you prefer, or simply cut off and thaw the amount you wish to serve and leave the rest in the freezer.

SERVES 12
200g (7oz) dark chocolate
   (39 per cent cocoa solids)
100g (4oz) caster sugar
6 tablespoons water
4 egg yolks
2 tablespoons brandy
600ml (1 pint) double cream

To decorate
12 large strawberries,
   hulled and sliced
A little single cream

PREPARE AHEAD
The torte can be frozen in the tin for up to 3 days. For longer freezing, once the torte is firmly frozen remove it from the tin, wrap in more clingfilm and seal in a plastic bag. Label and freeze for up to 3 months.

Oil a 20cm (8in) loose-bottomed or springform tin and line with clingfilm. Break the chocolate into sections and drop into a processor. Process for 1 minute or until just a few pieces remain in the otherwise powdery chocolate. Alternatively, finely grate the chocolate.

Measure the sugar and water into a small pan and heat gently until the sugar has dissolved, stirring occasionally. Now turn up the heat and boil briskly for 3–4 minutes to obtain a thin syrup.

Set the processor running and pour the hot syrup through the funnel on to the chocolate so it melts. Add just a little more boiling water if some unmelted chocolate remains. Next, add the egg yolks and process for a few seconds before adding the brandy. If you are not using a processor, beat the ingredients together.

In a separate bowl beat the cream to a soft, floppy consistency then fold in the chocolate mixture. Spread in the prepared tin, levelling the top with the back of a spoon, then cover with clingfilm and transfer to the freezer for a minimum of 6 hours to freeze.

Take the torte from the freezer 20 minutes before serving. Remove from the tin, strip away the clingfilm, put on a plate and leave to thaw; it should still be slightly frozen when it is cut into wedges for serving.

Place a wedge of chocolate torte in the centre and arrange a sliced strawberry around each serving. Drizzle a little cream over each portion, if liked, and serve immediately.

Canterbury Tart

This is our absolute favourite apple tart. A deep tart shell of crisp, buttery pastry filled with a magical mixture that is like tarte au citron combined with grated apples. It freezes well, too! To get a really crisp base to the tart, put a thick baking tray in the oven while it preheats, then when the tart bakes on top of it the base will be golden and crisp.

SERVES 10

For the pastry
100g (4oz) chilled butter, cubed
225g (8oz) plain flour
25g (1oz) icing sugar, sifted
1 egg, beaten
2 tablespoons water

For the filling
4 eggs
225g (8oz) caster sugar
Finely grated zest and juice
    of 2 lemons
100g (4oz) butter, melted
2 large cooking apples, peeled,
    cored and coarsley grated
2 red dessert apples, cored,
    quartered and thinly sliced
25g (1oz) demerara sugar

You will need a 28cm (11in) flan tin that's about 4cm deep. If making the pastry by hand, rub the butter into the flour and icing sugar until the mixture resembles breadcrumbs, then stir in the beaten egg and water and bring together to form a dough.

If using a processor, combine the flour, butter and icing sugar in the bowl, then process until the mixture resembles ground almonds. Pour in the beaten egg and water and pulse the blade until the dough starts to form a ball.

Roll out the pastry on a lightly floured work surface until slightly larger than the tin, then use a rolling pin to lift the pastry into the tin. Trim the edges and prick the base all over with a fork. Chill for 30 minutes.

Preheat the oven to 200°C/180°C fan/Gas 6. Prick the pastry in the tin with a fork then line with baking parchment and fill with baking beans. Bake blind for 20 minutes, then remove the beans and paper and return to the oven for another 10 minutes, until lightly golden and the base is cooked.

The pastry can be baked blind up to a day ahead. The filling can be prepared and kept covered at room temperature for up to 4 hours. To reheat, bake for about 20 minutes or until piping hot.

FREEZE
Freezes well, cooked, for up to a month.

AGA
There's no need to bake blind. Bake on the floor of the roasting oven for 25–30 minutes. If necessary, after 10 minutes slide the cold plain shelf on the second set of runners to prevent the pastry browning further. Transfer to the simmering oven to set the filling for about a further 10 minutes.

To prepare the filling, beat the eggs, sugar, lemon zest and juice together in a large mixing bowl. Stir in the warm melted butter, then the grated cooking apples and mix well. Arrange the sliced apples in a spiral over the top and sprinkle with the demerara sugar.

Bake for 30–35 minutes, or until the centre feels firm to the touch and the apple slices are tinged brown. Serve warm with cream.

Victorian Trifle

One of the surest signs of the success of a recipe is when people come back for more, and most of them eat embarrassing amounts of this trifle. It is truly luscious without being unduly rich, which is exactly what most people want nowadays. The trifle benefits from being made a day ahead; it sets and serves well and the Sherry can gently permeate throughout. If time is short use a tin of custard, then fold in 300ml (10fl oz) whipped cream to cheer it up.

SERVES 10

For the custard
3 egg yolks
25g (1oz) cornflour
50g (2oz) caster sugar
600ml (1 pint) milk
300ml (10fl oz) single cream

For the filling
16 trifle sponges
½ jar of strawberry jam
2 bought macaroons or 20 ratafias
1 × 800g tin pear halves in
   natural juice or light syrup
250ml (8fl oz) medium-dry Sherry
175g (6oz) red seedless grapes,
   halved

To decorate
150ml (5fl oz) whipping cream,
   or more if liked
50g (2oz) flaked almonds, toasted

You will need a shallow 2.25-litre
   (4-pint) glass bowl.

First, make the custard. Put the egg yolks, cornflour and sugar into a large bowl and stir together with a whisk. Heat the milk and cream together in a pan until hot but not boiling. Gradually whisk into the yolks, then return the mixture to the pan. Stir over a high heat until the mixture just comes to the boil and the custard thickens. Take off the heat, cover and allow to cool.

Split the sponges and spread generously with strawberry jam. Sandwich together and arrange in the base of the dish, close together, cutting to fit if necessary. Crumble the macaroons or ratafias over the top.

Combine 150ml (5fl oz) pear juice drained from the tin with the Sherry and sprinkle over the sponge and crumbled biscuits. Level the surface by pressing down with a spoon.

Drain the pears and cut each half in three lengthways and arrange over the sponges. Scatter the grapes on top. Spread the cooled custard over the fruit. Cover and leave until completely cold before transferring to the fridge to chill and set.

Beat the whipping cream until just stiff enough to hold a soft, floppy shape. Gently spread over the surface of the set custard and scatter with the almonds. Cover and chill until ready to serve.

PREPARE AHEAD
The made trifle can be covered with clingfilm and kept in the fridge for up to 2 days before serving.

Mincemeat & Apricot Streusel

Making a large pie and cutting it into serving pieces is a lot easier than making individual mince pies, and this version makes a welcome change to the usual mince pies around Christmas. Any other time of the year it can be made with Bramley apples instead of apricots, reserving the brandy for high days and holidays. If you are nervous making pastry, be reassured; this pastry, although rolled out thinly, just needs pushing around with your fingers to repair it. The streusel topping is made by coarsely grating a dough.

MAKES ABOUT 16 SLICES

For the filling
100g (4oz) ready-to-eat dried apricots, chopped
1 tablespoon brandy
Approx. 750g (1½lb) mincemeat

For the pastry base
175g (6oz) plain flour
1½ tablespoons icing sugar, sifted
100g (4oz) butter
A little cold water

For the topping
75g (3oz) butter
75g (3oz) self-raising flour
40g (1½oz) semolina
40 g (1½oz) caster sugar

To serve
A little icing sugar, sifted
Cream or brandy butter

Lightly grease a 23 × 33cm (13 × 9in) Swiss roll tin. Combine the apricots and brandy for the filling in a bowl so they can soak while the pastry is made.

Measure the flour and icing sugar for the pastry into a mixing bowl and rub in the butter until the mixture resembles coarse breadcrumbs. Add just sufficient water to mix to a firm dough that leaves the sides of the bowl clean. Or, if you prefer, make the pastry in a processor. If time allows, wrap the dough in clingfilm and chill for about 30 minutes.

Roll out the pastry to a rectangle slightly larger than the tin, then use to line the tin's base and sides. Do not worry if the pastry breaks or falls short in some places. Trim the pastry level with the top edges of the tin and use the off-cut pieces to patch and fill wherever necessary.

Mix the mincemeat with the apricots and brandy then spread over the pastry base. Preheat the oven to 200°C/180°C fan/Gas 6.

To make the topping, melt the butter in a small pan. Leave aside to cool while you measure the remaining ingredients into a bowl. Pour in the cooled butter and stir to form a soft dough. Using the coarse side of a grater, grate the dough evenly over the mincemeat. If the dough is too soft to grate, it means the butter was too hot when it was mixed into the dough, but this is easily put right: simply chill the dough for about 15 minutes and it will behave beautifully.

Cool and cut the streusel into slices and store in an airtight container in a cool place. Warm at 150°C/130°C fan/Gas 2 for about 20 minutes and dust with icing sugar just before serving.

Store the slices in a plastic freezer container. Seal and label, then freeze for up to 3 months.

Bake on the grid shelf in the roasting oven and position the cold plain shelf on the second set of runners. Bake the streusel for 10 minutes, then transfer to the floor of the roasting oven and bake for a further 15–20 minutes or until the streusel is a light golden brown.

For perfect pastry, cold hands, chilled fat, cold water and a cold rolling-out surface are best. The air trapped in the making of the dough will expand more if it is cold, making the pastry rise well. For this reason, too, chill pastry dough for about 30 minutes before baking.

Bake for about 20–25 minutes until pale golden brown. Check the streusel after 10–12 minutes and, if necessary, turn the tin so the mixture cooks evenly. Leave to cool in the tin until just warm. Before serving, dust with icing sugar and divide into slices. Delicious with cream or brandy butter at Christmas.

GREAT EATS TO GO WITH DRINKS

*

THE NIBBLES IN this chapter are some of my all-time favourites. I've tried to give a good selection of hot and cold canapés here, so that you can mix and match.

The Herb Cheese Toasts (page 216) are a staple – they require hardly any ingredients, you can make them ahead and store them in the fridge or freezer, and they can be baked in about 10 minutes from frozen. They are completely moreish and I always have a batch in the freezer just incase someone pops round for drinks.

Catering for a crowd can be tricky – the amount that people might eat at a drinks party can really vary depending on the time of day. For afterwork drinks, make sure you have plenty of food, but for drinks before a dinner, keep the nibbles to a minimum so people don't get too full. I think about five items per person should be offered in general and a selection of hot and cold, ideally. Serve alongside bowls of crisps, nuts and marinated olives, with lots of napkins.

Canapés should be the right size to be eaten in one bite – anything more gets a little tricky when standing and holding a drink at the same time! That's why Blinis (page 204) and cheesy biscuits are excellent finger foods.

Think about the occasion and season when choosing your drinks menu and always have a non-alcoholic option amongst your drinks. The Iced Wine Tea (page 223) is the perfect drink on a hot summer's day, while Winter Mulled Wine (page 225) is inextricably linked with Christmas for me.

The art of making homemade cordials and squashes seems to have been forgotten they make a lovely touch. Elderflower Cordial (page 222), made from elderflower blossom picked in early summer before the berries arrive, makes a fragrant, beautiful syrup for a summery refreshment. The other 'free' liqueur you can make is Sloe Gin (page 224).

Blinis

These are a Russian type of pancake traditionally made with buckwheat flour. I prefer to use a combination of plain and wholemeal flour for flavour and, for ease and speed, make the batter in a food processor. It is then left in a warm place to bubble away quietly for about 45 minutes, so you can then fold in a beaten egg white when you are ready. Here, I have adapted the recipe to make miniature versions.

175g (6oz) plain flour
50g (2oz) wholemeal flour
1 × 7g packet fast-action dried yeast
1 teaspoon salt
1 teaspoon sugar
300ml (10fl oz) warm milk
1 egg, separated
1 tablespoon melted butter, or cream

To serve
Soured cream
Snippets of smoked salmon
Chopped fresh dill
Salmon caviar or lumpfish roe

PREPARE AHEAD
The freshly cooked blini can be cooled and sealed in plastic bags. They can then be stored in the fridge for up to 2 days.

FREEZE
The blinis can be frozen for up to 2 months.

Put the dry ingredients into a food processor, then set the machine in motion. Pour in the warm milk then add the egg yolk and process until the mixture forms a smooth batter. Pour into a mixing bowl, cover with clingfilm, then a folded tea towel and leave aside in a warm place for 45 minutes.

Whisk the egg white until stiff but not dry. Fold the melted butter, or cream, into the batter followed by the egg white.

If you have a conventional pancake griddle, this would be ideal. If not, use a large, medium-weight, non-stick frying pan. Put the pan on a low to moderate heat and leave for several minutes. Wipe the surface with a piece of kitchen paper moistened with oil.

Now, using a tablespoon, pour some batter from the tip of the spoon into the pan (about 2cm/¾in diameter). This technique helps to keep the pancakes round.

After 1–2 minutes holes will appear in the surface of the batter; use a palette knife to flip the pancakes over then press them down on to the surface of the pan using the flat blade of the palette knife, just for 1–2 seconds. Cook for a further 1–2 minutes until browned, then transfer to a baking tray lined with kitchen paper to cool.

Top with seasoned soured cream, then snippets of smoked salmon and dill, or a little salmon caviar or lumpfish roe. Arrange on serving trays and serve slightly chilled.

AGA
The blinis can be cooked on the simmering plate. Lift the lid for 15 minutes to allow the plate to cool sufficiently, grease the plate and proceed as in the recipe.

Home-made Marinated Olives

I like to marinate olives, using the cheaper green olives in brine and making my own delicious oil. The marinating oil is also delicious used as a dressing on salads. Try different combinations of spices – cardamom seeds, bay leaves and pickling spice also all work well with the chilli and garlic.

1 jar of green or black pitted olives in brine
2 garlic cloves, peeled and bruised
1 fresh or dried chilli pepper, split in half
1 sprig of rosemary, basil or coriander
Mild olive oil, enough to refill the olive jar

Drain the olives from their brine and rinse them in cold water, but keep the jar. Put the olives back into the jar and refill with olive oil. Add the bruised garlic cloves, chilli and herbs. Keep in the fridge for two weeks to let the flavours mature. Add a few cubes of feta cheese, if liked, too.

Crudités

Crunchy, fresh vegetables are still a favourite at drinks parties and so easy to prepare. I serve celery batons, pepper slices, strips of carrot, small sprigs of cauliflower or broccoli, radishes, discs of cucumber, sugar snap peas, baby corn and strips of fresh fennel alongside Fresh Herb Sauce (page 249).

PREPARE AHEAD
All the veg can be prepared and kept in sealed plastic bags in the fridge up to 8 hours ahead of serving.

Parmesan & Paprika Nutters

These are quick and easy to make and utterly delicious. If you are nervous about using a piping bag, chill the mixture in the fridge until firm, then roll marble-size pieces of mixture between your hands instead. The result is just as good, but it does take a little longer.

MAKES ABOUT 40 BISCUITS

100g (4oz) very soft butter,
    warm but not runny
50g (2oz) semolina
85g (3 ½oz) self-raising flour
75g (3oz) freshly grated Parmesan
Salt and freshly ground black pepper
1 teaspoon mild paprika
Approx. 40 salted cashew nuts,
    for topping

Preheat the oven to 180°C/160°C/Gas 4. You will need two greased baking trays and a piping bag fitted with a plain 1cm (½in) nozzle.

Measure all the ingredients except the nuts into a large bowl and stir together until thoroughly mixed. This can be done in a processor, if you prefer. If the mixture is a little stiff, add a little more butter.

Transfer the biscuit mixture to the piping bag and pipe out small blobs of mixture, about 2cm (¾in) in diameter, spacing them regularly on the baking trays. Press a nut in the centre of each biscuit.

Bake for 12–15 minutes or until a pale golden brown, then cool on a wire rack.

PREPARE AHEAD
These biscuits can be made up to a week ahead, reheat in a low oven on the day to freshen up.

FREEZE
Freeze for up to 3 months.

AGA
Slide the baking sheet on to the lowest set of runners in the roasting oven with the cold plain shelf two sets above. Bake for 10–12 minutes, watching carefully, until pale golden brown.

Watercroft Flaky Cheese Biscuits

This recipe (photographed with parprika nutters on the previous page) are ideal to serve with drinks as they are small, crisp and piquant and relatively easy to make in party quantities. The off-cuts of pastry can be re-rolled and cut into extra-long cheese straws which look sensational served in tall containers on a buffet table. If you prefer to make cheese straws only, the method for making the pastry is slightly different and is given at the end of the biscuit recipe.

MAKES ABOUT 36 BISCUITS
350g (12oz) mature Cheddar,
    finely grated
1 tablespoon mustard powder
1 teaspoon salt
1 teaspoon freshly ground black pepper
1 × 375g pack frozen, ready-rolled
    puff pastry, thawed

Preheat the oven to 190°C/170°C fan/Gas 5. You will need two lightly greased baking trays.

Put the grated cheese into a large bowl with the mustard, salt and pepper and toss lightly together until well mixed; divide into four equal portions.

Position the roll of pastry parallel to the front edge of the work surface and unroll it away from you; the piece will measure about 35 × 23cm (14 × 9in). Sprinkle the top half of the pastry with a portion of cheese. Cut off the lower half and place directly over the top half to cover the cheese. Roll the pastry out until the strip regains its original size.

Repeat this process of sprinkling, covering and rolling the pastry 2 more times.

Now sprinkle the fourth and final portion of cheese on the pastry block, cut in half and cover the cheese with the left-hand side. You will now have a block of pastry/cheese measuring about 18 × 11.5 × 2.5cm. Press the layers together firmly. Trim off any uneven or unmatched edges and keep the trimmings.

Take a large, sharp knife and cut into 5mm wide strips. Turn these flat on to the work surface and cut into 2.5cm long pieces. Transfer the pieces to the baking trays so the biscuits bake cut-side up. The last slice is difficult to cut, so don't bother; gather it together with the pastry trimmings and put on one side.

Bake the biscuits for about 8 minutes, but I advise you to watch them carefully during the last 2–3 minutes. They should be a good orange/brown for maximum crispness and flavour, but ovens vary and these biscuits over-brown very quickly so until you know exactly how long they will take in your oven, watch them carefully, then after that, time them exactly!

Use a palette knife to remove the biscuits to a wire rack. You will need to bake several batches, so after removing the baked biscuits from a baking tray, wipe it with kitchen paper and leave it to cool before using again.

Roll out the pastry trimmings to a long narrow strip slightly longer than your baking trays then cut the pastry lengthways into strips about 1 cm wide. Gently twist each strip about 6 times and arrange down the full length of the baking trays. Bake as above.

TO MAKE CHEESE STRAWS

Follow the above method to the stage of sprinkling on the third portion of cheese and covering this with the lower half of pastry. Now continue to roll out the pastry to its original size, then sprinkle half with the fourth and final portion of cheese. Cut in half and cover the cheese with the top half and roll out for the final time so that the pastry is 3–5 mm thick. Cut into strips as described above, making them as long as the length of the baking trays will allow. Bake as above, then leave on the trays for about 5 minutes before carefully removing to the wire rack to finish cooling. They are rather fragile.

Hot & Spicy Chicken Bites

Serve these skewers hot as a canapé with drinks. (Soaking the skewers in water prevents them from burning.)

MAKES 12
1 boneless, skinless chicken breast
1 tablespoon sweet chilli sauce
1 tablespoon soy sauce
1 good teaspoon red Thai curry paste
Salt and freshly ground black pepper
2 tablespoons sunflower oil

PREPARE AHEAD
Can be made up to a day ahead and marinated for up to 12 hours. You can also cook these skewers up to a day ahead and reheat to serve.

FREEZE
Freezes well, marinated and uncooked for up to 2 months.

AGA
Fry in a pan on the boiling plate or in a roasting tray on the floor of the roasting oven.

You will need 12 wooden cocktail skewers, soaked in water if you've not used them before. Slice the chicken breast into 12 thin strips.

Measure the sweet chilli sauce, soy sauce and Thai paste into a small bowl and stir together. Season with a little salt and pepper. Add the chicken strips and leave to marinate in the fridge for a minimum of 1 hour or overnight.

Thread the marinated chicken strips on to cocktail skewers.

Heat the oil in a non-stick frying pan. Fry the chicken skewers for about 5 minutes, turning the skewers around so they are golden brown all over and cooked through. Serve hot.

Cottage Pie Canapés

These are simply mini versions of a large cottage pie with a filo-pastry base – everyone's favourite.

MAKES 36
Approx. 5 sheets of filo pastry
Melted butter

For the mince
1 tablespoon sunflower oil
1 onion, finely chopped
250g (9oz) minced beef
2 tablespoons plain flour
75ml (3fl oz) red wine
150ml (¼ pint) beef stock
1 teaspoon tomato purée
1 teaspoon redcurrant jelly
½ teaspoon Worcestershire sauce
A dash of gravy browning
Salt and freshly ground black pepper
450g (1lb) King Edward potatoes,
     peeled and cubed
A knob of butter
2 tablespoons milk
50g (2oz) Parmesan, finely grated

PREPARE AHEAD
The pies can be made up
to 6 hours ahead, up to the
final baking stage.

FREEZE
The pies freeze well without
the potato topping.

AGA
Cook the mince in the
simmering oven for 45
minutes. To serve, cook on the
second set of runners in the
roasting oven for 12 minutes.

You will need three 12-hole mini muffin tins, greased with melted butter.Lay the filo pastry flat on a board and brush each sheet with melted butter, then lay them in a neat pile. Using a ruler, measure a square of 24 × 24cm (9½ × 9½in) and then cut the square into sixteen 6cm (2½in) squares to give 80 squares in total. Place two squares of filo into each muffin hole to make a case. Repeat until you have lined all 36 holes (you will have a few squares left over). Chill in the fridge.

Heat the oil in a frying pan, add the onion and fry for 5 minutes. Add the beef and fry, stirring, until brown. Sprinkle in the flour and stir to coat. Blend in the red wine and stock until the sauce is thickened, then stir in the purée, redcurrant jelly, Worcestershire sauce and gravy browning.

Season with salt and pepper, bring to the boil, cover and simmer for about 45 minutes to 1 hour until the mince is cooked. Spoon into a bowl and set aside to cool.

Put the potatoes into cold salted water, bring to the boil and boil for 15 minutes until tender. Mash with a knob of butter and the milk, season with salt and pepper and mash until smooth. Preheat the oven to 200°C/180°C fan/Gas 6.

Spoon a teaspoon of mince into the cases so they are half full. Spoon the mash on top and spread to the edges. Sprinkle with Parmesan and bake for 12–15 minutes until crisp and golden on top and the pastry is cooked. Serve warm.

Crostini With Dolcelatte & Fresh Figs

The blue cheese and fig combination of these little crostini is delicious. They are best served warm.

MAKES 20

1 small, thin baguette
25g (1oz) butter, softened
125g (4½oz) Dolcelatte
4 fresh figs
Sunflower oil, for brushing

PREPARE AHEAD
The crostini can be assembled up to 4 hours ahead and then cooked to serve.

AGA
Bake on the floor of the roasting oven for 7 minutes.

Preheat the oven to 220°C/200°C fan/Gas 7. Line a baking sheet with baking parchment.

Slice the baguette diagonally into 20 thin slices and butter one side of each slice. Arrange, buttered-side down, on the baking sheet.

Slice the cheese into 20 cubes and place one cube on top of each slice of bread. Spread slightly with a knife.

Top and tail the figs, slice in half through the stalk and then slice each half into 5 wedges. You will end up with 40 thin wedges of fig.

Arrange two slices of fig on each crostini and brush very lightly with oil. Bake in the oven for 8–10 minutes or until the cheese is just melted and golden – watch carefully.
Serve warm.

Herb Cheese Toasts

Simple and delicious – the sort of 'nibble' that everybody loves. My only advice is to make plenty! See previous page for photograph.

MAKES 18–24 TOASTS
1 long thin baguette
Softened butter, for spreading
1 × 125g tub full-fat cream cheese
    with herbs and garlic
Approx. 175g (6oz) Cheddar, grated
A little mild paprika

Preheat the oven to 220°C/200°C fan/Gas 7. Lightly grease two baking trays.

Take a sharp bread knife and cut the baguette diagonally into 1cm (½ in) thick slices. Thinly butter both sides of each slice, then spread the cream cheese on one side. Top each with a little grated cheese and a dusting of paprika.

Arrange on the prepared baking trays and bake for 8–10 minutes or until melted and golden brown.

PREPARE AHEAD
The toasts can be prepared before baking, arranged on the baking trays, covered in clingfilm and kept in the fridge for up to 2 days.

FREEZE
Freezes well uncooked for up to 2 months.

AGA
Bake on the floor of the roasting oven for 8–10 minutes or until golden brown.

Smoked Salmon, Prawn & Dill Canapés

These are so pretty to look at and fresh and healthy to eat – the mayonnaise adds a little flavour and holds the prawn in place. To make them really smart, and if you do not want to serve the bread, arrange 20 Chinese spoons on a serving plate, spoon a teaspoon of mayonnaise on each one and sit a canapé on top. (See page 218 for a photo.)

MAKES 20

4 large slices of smoked salmon
20 cooked and peeled king prawns
2 tablespoons light mayonnaise
20 sprigs of fresh dill
Juice of ½ a lemon
5 slices of rye bread
Soft butter, for spreading
Freshly ground black pepper

Lay the salmon slices on a board and slice into twenty 10 × 1.5cm (4 × ¾in) strips.

Sit a prawn in the centre of a strip of salmon (so the top and tail are sticking out). Spoon a little mayonnaise on top of the prawn, lay a piece of dill on top and sprinkle with black pepper. Roll the smoked salmon piece around the prawn and squeeze over a little lemon juice. Repeat with the remaining ingredients to give 20 canapés.

Spread the bread slices with butter, cut off the crusts and cut each slice into four squares. Arrange on a plate, sit the prawn canapé on each square, sprinkle with black pepper and a squeeze of lemon and serve cold.

PREPARE AHEAD
Can be made completely up to 6 hours ahead.

Miniature Cocktail Quiches

This is a quick, easy way to make a party quantity of bite-size quiches and serve them hot. Making one large quiche in a baking tray then cutting it out into miniature rounds is far quicker and less fiddly than making individual tiny quiches, so for me the cutting-out technique wins hands down.

MAKES ABOUT 60

225g (8oz) ready-made shortcrust pastry

For the filling
12 rashers of streaky bacon, rind removed
1 large onion, finely chopped
300ml (10fl oz) double cream
3 eggs
Salt and freshly ground black pepper

PREPARE AHEAD
The quiches can be prepared and cooked about 6 hours ahead of serving.

FREEZE
Freeze the whole cooked quiche for up to 1 month.

AGA
Cook the quiche on the floor of the roasting oven with the cold plain shelf above after 10 minutes until the pastry is brown and the filling set, about 20–25 minutes. Cool and stamp out rounds as in the recipe. To reheat the mini quiches, place them on a baking tray on the floor of the roasting oven for 8–10 minutes.

Preheat the oven to 190°C/170°C/Gas 5 and put in a flat baking tray to heat up. Lightly grease a large Swiss roll tin measuring 33 × 23cm (13 × 9in).

Roll out the pastry thinly and use to line the base and sides of the Swiss roll tin. Trim away and discard the excess pastry from the top rim of the tin, then transfer the tin to the freezer while you make the filling.

Cut the bacon rashers across into thin strips. Heat a non-stick frying pan and cook the bacon strips without browning them until the fat starts to run. Stir in the onion, cover and cook over a low heat for about 10 minutes, stirring occasionally, until the onion is softened but not coloured. Remove from the heat and leave to cool.

Combine the cream, eggs, bacon and onion together in a bowl and beat together with a wire whisk. Taste and season with salt and pepper.

Remove the pastry-lined Swiss roll tin from the freezer, prick the base all over with a fork and put it on top of the preheated baking tray in the oven. Carefully pour in the quiche filling, then bake for about 30 minutes or until puffed and golden. Leave the Swiss roll tin on top of a wire rack to cool.

When ready, the quiche can be cut into rounds using a 3.5cm (1¼in) plain cutter. Arrange them on a baking tray and reheat in the oven at 220°C/200°C/ Gas 7 for 10–15 minutes or until tinged golden and piping hot. Serve immediately.

Cider Punch

Chill everything well. For a slightly less alcoholic and very refreshing drink, omit the brandy and add a litre bottle of chilled lemonade.

MAKES 14 GLASSES
1 litre (1¾ pints) medium dry cider
1 bottle of dry white wine
1 wine glass of medium Sherry
    (approx. 150ml/5fl oz)
1 wine glass of brandy
    (approx. 150ml/5fl oz)

To serve
1 lemon, thinly sliced
1 red-skinned apple, sliced
1 small, thin-skinned orange, sliced

Combine all the liquid ingredients together in a large glass jug.

Have the glasses ready with the fruit divided among them. Pour and serve.

PREPARE AHEAD
The drink can be made and kept covered in the fridge for up to a day ahead.

Sparkling Wine Cup

Make sure that all bottles and fruit are chilled well ahead of time. If you do not have orange liqueur, you could use brandy instead.

MAKES 18 GLASSES
½ a ripe melon, deseeded and cubed
225g (8oz) fresh strawberries, hulled and sliced
24 ice cubes
2 bottles of Sauternes, chilled
1 litre (1¾ pints) lemonade
1 wine glass of orange liqueur, such as
    Cointreau, curaçao, or Grand Marnier
    (approx. 150ml/5fl oz)
Juice of 1 lemon

To serve
18 sprigs of fresh mint

Put some of the fruit in a large glass jug with six ice cubes and divide the rest of the fruit and ice between the glasses.

Pour the chilled wine, lemonade, liqueur and lemon juice into the jug, stir and it's ready to serve. Pop a sprig of mint into each glass just before handing them to your guests.

PREPARE AHEAD
This drink is best drunk freshly made when it has some fizz.

TIP
If serving drinks such as Pimms or fruit cup on a hot day, put the fruit and ice straight into the glasses arranged on a tray. It is then much easier to pour the liquid into the glasses and serve.

Elderflower Cordial

This is made using elderflower blossom, which flowers in early summer but I've discovered that the blossom can be successfully frozen in plastic bags. The heads are then added, still frozen, to the hot syrup to make a cordial tasting exactly the same as one made with fresh flowers. (Don't defrost the flowers otherwise they turn brown.) Citric acid is no problem; the white crystals, resembling sugar, can be bought from all chemists. Dilute the cordial with sparkling or still water or add a little to a fruit salad for an extra layer of flavour.

MAKES APPROX. 2.9 LITRES
(5¼ PINTS)
1.5kg (3½lb) caster sugar
1.5 litres (2½ pints) water
3 lemons
Approx. 25 elderflower heads
50g (2oz) citric acid

To serve
Chilled carbonated water
Ice cubes

Measure the sugar and water into a large pan. Bring to the boil, stirring, until the sugar has dissolved. Remove from the heat and leave to cool.

Slice the lemons thinly either by hand or using the thin slicing disc in a processor. Put the slices in a large plastic box or glass bowl. Add the elderflower heads and citric acid and pour in the cool sugar syrup. Cover and leave overnight.

The following day, strain the syrup, decant into sterilized bottles, seal and store in the fridge.

To serve, dilute to taste with chilled carbonated water and serve with ice.

PREPARE AHEAD
The cordial can be made, bottled and stored in the fridge for 4–6 weeks. It also freezes well, too.

Iced Wine Tea

This is an excellent thirst-quencher on a hot afternoon instead of tea! Add a sprig of mint to each glass. It is essential to serve it very cold.

MAKES 10 GLASSES
2 teaspoons Darjeeling tea
600ml (1 pint) boiled water
1 bottle dry white wine, chilled
A few parings of orange zest
A few sprigs of fresh mint
Ice cubes (optional)

PREPARE AHEAD
The made drink can be kept covered in the fridge for up to 1 day.

Warm the teapot in the usual way, then spoon the tea into the pot. Pour in the freshly boiled water, stir, cover and leave to brew for 2–3 minutes. Strain the tea into a jug, cool, then chill in the fridge.

Combine the tea and wine in a chilled jug and add the orange parings and fresh mint. Serve with ice if you wish.

ICED TEA

Iced tea is not too fattening, is thirst quenching and very easy to make. Use a fragrant loose tea and make a rather weak infusion by stirring the leaves into a jug of cold water. Leave overnight in the fridge, then strain. Lemon juice and sugar can be added just before serving. For extra chill, freeze some of the tea in ice-cube trays.

ICED COFFEE

For the very best iced coffee, use good-quality ground coffee and dilute the coffee to taste with ice-cold milk. Add cream or ice cubes, if liked. I usually keep a jug of iced coffee made up in the fridge in very hot weather, and serve in small glasses.

Sloe Gin

Sloes are related to apricots, cherries, peaches, nectarines and plums, but are very sour. They need to be picked when they are ripe in the autumn, but you don't have to start making the sloe gin there and then because the fruits can be frozen and used when it suits you. After marinating in sugar and gin for 6 months, though, the liquid becomes a warm red with a rich flavour, somewhere between blackcurrants and cherry brandy, with a hint of almond. Delicious! You may well not be able to wait 6 months to try!

MAKES 2 LITRES
About 1kg (2¼lb) sloes
225–275g (8–10oz) caster sugar
about 1 litre of gin
You'll need 2 sterilized 1-litre bottles.

FREEZE
Freeze the clean, dry sloes in a plastic box for up to 1 year. Once thawed, the berries will not need pricking, just pack them into bottles with any juices that have accumulated during thawing.

Wash the sloes, remove the stalks and snip or prick each sloe to make the juices run. Take a clean, empty gin bottle, or similar, and fill two-thirds full with snipped sloes. To each bottle, add 225–275g (8–10oz) caster sugar (depending on how sweet you'd like your gin to be), then fill the bottle up with gin. Put the lid on and shake well.

Put on one side for at least 2 months before using, shaking the bottle once or twice a week. In theory, you should not drink it for at least 6 months to experience the flavour at its rich and redolent best! After 6 months, strain the sloes from the gin and discard them (don't eat the sloe berries).

Rebottle the strained sloe gin in small bottles and give as gifts – if you can bear to part with it!

Serve in small glasses as you would a liqueur as an after-dinner drink.

Winter Mulled Wine

For an extra kick on a winter's day, add a Sherry glass of brandy just before serving.

MAKES 12 GLASSES
4 lemons
2 large oranges
2 bottles of red wine
1.2 litres (2 pints) water
16 cloves
2 cinnamon sticks
100–175g (4–6oz) caster sugar

PREPARE AHEAD
The mulled wine can be made, strained, cooled and kept in covered jugs in the fridge for up to 3 days. Reheat and add the quartered slices of lemon and orange just before serving.

FREEZE
Freezes the leftovers for up to 6 months.

AGA
Bring to the boil on the boiling plate, cover and transfer to the simmering oven for about an hour.

Peel the zest very thinly from two lemons and one orange. Thinly slice one of the remaining lemons and the remaining orange, then quarter the slices, put on a plate, cover and reserve for a garnish. Squeeze the juice from the remaining three whole lemons and the zested orange.

Pour the wine, water and citrus juices into a large pan and add the cloves and cinnamon sticks. Bring to simmering point, then cover and keep just below that heat for 1 hour.

Stir in sugar to taste, then strain and serve hot with the reserved orange and lemon slices floating on top.

TIME
FOR TEA

*

Bakes for morning coffee, fetes,
fairs and proper afternoon tea

I COULDN'T REVISE *At Home* without adding a baking chapter – it wouldn't be complete! So, this new edition has an entire chapter devoted to cakes, bakes and sweet treats.

Baking is more scientific that other cooking so use a good set of scales (I prefer digital), check your oven temperature is correct and make adjustments if your cake is cooking too quickly or needs more time.

Choose imperial or metric measures and don't mix the two – this is particularly important with baking – and if you've not made something before, please have a trial run before making it for an occasion, just incase you need to make some tweaks.

Parents, the Simple Lemon Traybake and Banana & Chocolate Chip Cupcakes (pages 228 and 242) are perfect for school fairs or for cheering up tired children after school.

Make the Double Divine Chocolate Cake or Date & Walnut Traybake (pages 232 and 229) to serve with morning coffee (take them into work and you'll be very popular).

And then, for a proper afternoon tea – to celebrate an occasion or simply to add a special touch of indulgence to an afternoon with the girls – there are some dainty specials to try, including my Mini Victoria Sandwiches (page 238), Buttermilk Sultana Scones (page 230) and Mini Meringues (page 239).

Simple Lemon Traybake

Traybakes are the most versatile of cakes, easy and simple to make – and lemon is my all-time favourite. This makes a shallow traybake hence just 12 pieces.

CUTS INTO 12 SQUARES

For the cake
120g (4½oz) baking spread
120g (4½oz) caster sugar
175g (6oz) self-raising flour
2 eggs
1 teaspoon baking powder
3 tablespoons milk
Finely grated zest of 1 lemon

For the topping
100g (4oz) sugar
Juice of 1 lemon

PREPARE AHEAD
Wrap the cooled cake, still with the foil lining attached, in clingfilm. Chill for up to 1 week.

FREEZE
Remove the foil lining from the cooled cake and wrap closely in clingfilm. Seal inside a plastic bag, label and freeze for up to 3 months.

You will need a 4cm deep roasting tin or tray-bake tin that measures 30 × 23cm (12 × 9in). Turn the tin upside down and mould a strip of foil around the base and sides. Turn the tin the right way up and drop the foil lining into the tin. Brush with a little oil.

Preheat the oven to 180°C/160°C fan/Gas 4.

Measure the cake ingredients into a large bowl and beat for about 2 minutes until smooth. Turn the mixture into the lined tin and level the top with the back of a spoon.

Bake for 20–25 minutes or until the cake is golden brown and shows signs of shrinking away from the sides. Press the centre lightly with your fingertips; it should be slightly resistant to the pressure. Remove the cake from the oven.

Mix together the sugar and lemon juice for the topping and brush over the surface of the hot cake. Leave the cake in the tin until barely warm, then use the foil lining to lift it from the tin on to a wire rack.

Cut into 12 pieces and serve warm or cold.

AGA
Bake on the lowest set of runners in the roasting oven and slide the cold plain shelf on to the second set of runners. Bake for 20–25 minutes, turning once during cooking.

Date & Walnut Traybake

A traybake is such a good cake to feed lots of people. No icing is needed for this recipe – it's just lovely as it is.

SERVES 20

250g (9oz) dates, chopped

100g (4oz) butter

350ml (12fl oz) boiling water

3 eggs

100g (7oz) light muscovado sugar

75g (3oz) walnuts, chopped

300g (12oz) self-raising flour

2 teaspoons baking powder

½ teaspoon ground cinnamon

PREPARE AHEAD
The traybake can be made up to a day ahead.

FREEZE
It freezes well.

AGA
Bake on the grid shelf on the floor of the roasting oven, with the cold sheet on the second set of runners, for 35–40 minutes.

Preheat the oven to 180°C/160°C fan/Gas 4. Grease a 30 × 23cm (12 × 9in) traybake tin and line with baking parchment.

Measure the dates and butter into a bowl. Pour over the boiling water and set aside to cool.

In a separate bowl, mix the eggs and sugar together and beat until smooth. Add the date mixture and the remaining ingredients. Mix until smooth and pour into the tin.

Bake in the preheated oven for 35–40 minutes until golden brown and shrinking away from the sides of the tin. Leave to cool then cut into 20 pieces to serve.

Buttermilk & Sultana Scones

Buttermilk gives a lovely, light texture to these scones. Omit the sultanas if you prefer plain scones.

MAKES 12

450g (1lb) self-raising flour
2 heaped teaspoons baking powder
75g (3oz) butter, cubed
75g (3oz) caster sugar
100g (4oz) sultanas
2 large eggs, beaten
1 × 284ml carton buttermilk

To serve
Cream
Jam

PREPARE AHEAD
The scones are best made on the day, but they can be made up to a day ahead and reheated.

FREEZE
They freeze well cooked.

AGA
Bake on the grid shelf on the floor of the roasting oven with the cold sheet on the second set of runners for about 12 minutes.

Preheat the oven to 200°C/200°C fan/Gas 7. Line a baking sheet with baking parchment.

Measure the flour, baking powder and butter into a bowl. Rub with your fingertips until the mixture looks like breadcrumbs. Stir in the sugar and sultanas or do this in a food processor.

Mix the eggs and buttermilk together in a jug and pour all but 1 tablespoon into the flour bowl and lightly mix together until combined – it should be a fairly moist dough.

Lightly sprinkle the worktop with flour and gently knead the dough until smooth and soft. Roll the dough to about 2.5cm (1in) thick. Using a 6cm round fluted scone cutter, stamp out 12 scones.

Arrange the scones on the baking sheet and brush the tops with the reserved egg and milk mixture. Bake in the preheated oven for about 12–15 minutes until risen and lightly golden.

Double Divine Chocolate Cake

A moist chocolate cake that really can't go wrong and keeps well. It has a wonderful white chocolate icing so the contrast looks stunning, too.

SERVES 6

6½oz (190g) self-raising flour
2 level tablespoons cocoa powder
1 level teaspoon bicarbonate of soda
1 level teaspoon baking powder
5oz (150g) caster sugar
2 tablespoons golden syrup
2 eggs
¼ pint (150ml) sunflower oil
¼ pint (150ml) milk

Icing
200g Belgian white chocolate
150ml (¼ pint) double cream
1 × 125g tub full-fat cream cheese

PREPARE AHEAD
The cake is best made on the day but will keep in the fridge for up to 2 days.

FREEZE
It freezes well not iced or filled for up to 3 months.

AGA
Bake on the grid shelf on the floor of the roasting oven with the cold sheet on the second set of runners for about 20–30 minutes.

Heat the oven to 180°C/160°fan/Gas 4. Grease and line with greased greaseproof paper the bases of two 20cm (8-inch) straight-sided loose-bottomed sandwich tins.

Sift the dry ingredients into a large bowl and make a well in the centre. Add the syrup, eggs, oil and milk, mix with an electric hand whisk and pour into the tins. Bake in the oven for 25-30 minutes, or until the cake springs back when lightly pressed with your fingertips. Turn out on to a wire rack, remove the paper and leave to cool.

For the icing, break the white chocolate into a bowl. Heat the double cream in a pan until hot and pour the hot cream over the white chocolate to melt it. Stir until melted, then set aside to cool. Spoon the cream cheese into a bowl, gradually add the white chocolate mixture and beat until combined. Set aside to cool a little until thick enough to ice.

Spread half the icing on one cake, sit the other cake on top and spread the remaining icing on top to give a pretty finish.

'Proper' Sandwiches

In Suppers for Crowds, we talked about open sandwiches, which are quick to make for large groups of guests (see page 128), but 'closed sandwiches' make a lovely, smart, savoury addition to any afternoon tea.

BREADS & QUANTITIES

I use thinly sliced brown or white bread, which average about 24 slices. Allow one sandwich per person, if serving with scones and cake too, and a choice of two fillings. Always taste the filling before you put it in the bread. Flavour is very important – cucumber needs plenty of pepper, for instance.

For afternoon tea, cut the sandwiches into four triangles or three long fingers, and cut off the crusts first, as below, to give a more elegant finish. Small, bite-sized sandwiches look best served alongside scones, mini tarts and slices of cake.

IDEAS FOR AFTERNOON TEA

The following serving suggestions are favourites of mine – nothing unusual or ground-breaking! But for afternoon tea, simple, classic flavours are best.

Egg Mayonnaise, Mustard & Cress: Finely chopped hard-boiled eggs mixed with mayonnaise and a little Dijon, salt and pepper. Spread on a bread slice, then scatter with cress before covering with the second slice.

Curried Egg Mayonnaise: Follow the above method, but omit the mustard and add a little chopped mango chutney and a little curry powder or paste to taste.

The sandwiches can be made the night before, or in the morning before an afternoon event. Butter the bread, fill and stack no more than six sandwiches on top of each other. Put them, uncut, on large trays, cover completely with clingfilm, then a damp tea towel. Transfer to the fridge.

No more than 2 hours before serving, trim the crusts from the bread using a very sharp knife, then cut each sandwich into either 4 triangles or 4 domino shapes.

FOR A BUFFET
Arrange one kind of sandwich on each plate or tray, but if handing around, arrange a selection of all the sandwiches on large plates.

Cucumber: If making the day before, use slightly thicker slices of cucumber and lemon-flavoured butter. Season with black pepper.

Roasted Vegetable: Spread cream cheese over sliced bread and top with chopped chargrilled peppers, onions and aubergine.

Smoked Salmon: Buy the cheaper salmon trimmings, finely chop and add black pepper and lemon juice. If the salmon is too salty, mix with a little cream cheese or use unsalted butter.

Lemon Chicken: Mix mayonnaise with a little lemon juice and chopped fresh tarragon. Spread on the bread and top with sliced cooked chicken and romaine lettuce.

Goat's Cheese & Rocket: Spread soft goat's cheese and mango chutney on the bread and top with rocket.

Pastrami & Gherkin: Spread the bread with mayonnaise and mustard and top with pastrami and slices of gherkin.

Pâté & Pickle: Spread the bread with chicken liver pâté and top with chopped Cucumber & Dill Pickle (see page 15).

Crab & Chilli: Spread the bread with mayonnaise and top with crabmeat mixed with sweet chilli dipping sauce.

See also page 253 for some general advice on bread, spreads and filling quantities.

Mini Victoria Sandwiches

These individual Victoria sandwiches are easy to eat – and just a little bit different.

MAKES 12

2 large eggs
125g (4oz) self-raising flour
125g (4oz) soft butter
125g (4oz) caster sugar
1 level teaspoon baking powder
6 tablespoons strawberry jam
200ml (7fl oz) double cream, whipped
Extra caster sugar, for dusting

PREPARE AHEAD
These are best made on the day. The sponge can be baked up to a day ahead and assembled up to 4 hours ahead.

FREEZE
Freezes well unfilled.

AGA
Bake on the grid shelf on the floor of the roasting oven with the cold sheet on the second set of runners for 12–15 minutes.

Preheat the oven to 180°C/160°C fan/Gas 3. Grease a 12-hole straight sided muffin tin.

Measure the eggs, flour, butter, sugar and baking powder into a bowl. Whisk or beat until combined and smooth. Spoon into the muffin tin and level the tops with the back of a teaspoon.

Bake for 15 minutes or until well risen, pale golden and shrinking away from the sides. Leave for 10 minutes. Carefully remove from the tin and cool on a wire rack.

Slice each cake in half across the middle, spread the base slice with jam and cream and place the other half on top. Dust with caster sugar and serve.

Mini Meringues

Meringues are a wonderful dessert and handy to have in the cake tin ready to fill.

MAKES ABOUT 30
3 egg whites
175g (6oz) caster sugar

To serve
150ml (¼ pint) double cream, whipped
Fresh raspberries or strawberries

PREPARE AHEAD
The meringues can be make up to two months ahead and kept in a bag or box.

FREEZE
They freeze well in a box (this avoids crushing).

AGA
Slide the baking sheet anywhere in the simmering oven and bake for about 1 hour 10 minutes or until the meringues are just firm to the touch and can be easily removed from the paper.

Preheat the oven to 140°C/120°C fan/Gas 1. Line a baking sheet with baking parchment. You will need a piping bag with a 1cm (½in) plain nozzle.

Measure the egg whites into a large bowl (or the bowl of a free-standing machine). Whisk on high speed until white and fluffy, like a cloud. Still whisking on maximum speed, gradually add the sugar, a teaspoon at a time, until incorporated and the meringue is stiff and shiny and stands upright on the whisk.

Using the piping bag, pipe the meringue mixture into tiny rounds on the baking sheet – make sure they are the same size so they cook evenly.

Bake for about 45 minutes, or until the meringues come off the baking parchment easily. Remove from the paper on to a cooling rack and set aside until stone cold.

Keep in the cake tin until ready to serve with whipped cream and raspberries, strawberries or other soft fruits.

Mini Raspberry Tartlets

For a posh afternoon tea, these are for you! Chilling the pastry cases well means they will keep their shape and the shrinking of the pastry will be minimal.

MAKES 12

For the pastry
100g (4oz) plain flour
25g (1oz) icing sugar
50g (2oz) butter, cubed
1 large egg, beaten

For the crème patissière
2 eggs
25g (1oz) caster sugar
25g (1oz) plain flour
1 teaspoon vanilla extract
200ml (7fl oz) milk

For the decoration
300g (10oz) raspberries
Approx. 6 tablespoons redcurrant jelly

PREPARE AHEAD
The tartlets can be made up to 8 hours ahead.

FREEZE
The cooked pastry cases freeze well.

AGA
Cook the pastry case on the floor of the roasting oven for 8 minutes.

Preheat the oven to 180°C/160°C fan/Gas 4. You will need a 24-hole mini muffin tin.

To make the pastry, measure the flour, sugar and butter into a processor and whizz until like breadcrumbs. Add the egg and whizz again until it comes together to form a dough.

Lightly knead the pastry on a floured work surface and roll out thinly. Using a round cutter, cut out the pastry and use to line the tin(s). Chill for at least 30 minutes.

Prick the base of the tarts and bake for 8–10 minutes until golden brown, crisp and cooked. Set aside to cool.

To make the crème patissière, measure the eggs, sugar, flour and vanilla into a bowl. Add 1 tablespoon of milk and whisk using a hand whisk until smooth.

Heat the remaining milk in a pan until just simmering. Pour over the egg mixture and whisk quickly until combined. Wash the saucepan, pour in the mixture and heat over a medium heat until thickened, stirring all the time. Do not overheat otherwise the eggs will scramble. Set aside to cool.

Spoon the crème patissière into the pastry cases and arrange on a serving plate. Sit 3 or 4 raspberries on the top of each tart. Heat the redcurrant jelly until melted and runny and brush over the raspberries.

Chill until needed.

Banana & Chocolate Chip Cupcakes

These are great for breakfast or teatime.

MAKES 12

For the cakes
100g (4oz) butter, softened
2 eggs
175g (6oz) caster sugar
225g (8oz) self-raising flour
1 teaspoon baking powder
3 tablespoons milk
2 very ripe bananas, mashed
50g (2oz) chocolate chips

For the icing
50g (2oz) dark chocolate
  (39 per cent cocoa solids), melted

PREPARE AHEAD
The cakes can be made up
to a day ahead.

FREEZE
They freeze well cooked for
up to 3 months.

AGA
Bake on the grid shelf on
the floor of the roasting oven
with the cold sheet on the
second set of runners for
20–25 minutes.

Preheat the oven to 180°C/160°C fan/Gas 4. Line a 12-hole muffin tin with paper cases.

Measure the butter, eggs, caster sugar, flour, baking powder, milk and bananas into a bowl and beat together until combined and smooth. Mix in the chocolate chips.

Spoon into the paper cases and bake for about 25 minutes until well risen, golden brown and shrinking away from the cases. Remove the cases from the tin and set aside to cool.

Drizzle over the melted chocolate in a zigzag pattern using a small piping bag or teaspoon.

Cornish Sticky Cake

This recipe was given to us by a colleague's mother who thought we would like it, and she was right. We have tweaked it and made it our own – we hope you enjoy it.

MAKES 1 × 900G (2LB) LOAF

For the fruit layer
1 tablespoon golden syrup
50g (2oz) butter
25g (1oz) brown sugar
40g (1½oz) flaked almonds
40g (1½ oz) glacé cherries, quartered
25g (1oz) sultanas
25g (1oz) stem ginger,
    cut into small pieces

For the sponge mixture
175g (6oz) soft butter
175g (6oz) caster sugar
3 eggs
175g (6oz) self-raising flour
1½ teaspoon baking powder
1 heaped tablespoon
    ground ginger

Preheat the oven to 180°C/160°C fan/Gas 4. Grease and line a 900g (2lb) loaf tin.

To make the fruit layer, measure the syrup, butter and sugar into a pan. Gently heat, stirring, until just melted. Add the almonds, cherries, sultanas and ginger pieces and stir until combined. Spoon into the base of the tin.

To make the sponge, measure all the ingredients into a bowl. Beat together until smooth and combined. Spoon on top of the fruit layer in the tin and spread out evenly.

Bake for 45 minutes until well risen and lightly golden. Leave to cool for 5 minutes, then tip upside down and remove the paper. Cut into slices to serve.

PREPARE AHEAD
Can be made up to a
day ahead.

FREEZE
Freezes well cooked for up
to 3 months.

AGA
The cake is best made in two 450g (1lb) tins. Sit these in a large roasting tin and bake on the lowest set of runners in the roasting oven for 35 minutes. Watch carefully as you may need to place a cold sheet on the second set of runners.

Orange Cake

Simple orange cake – moist, light with a slightly nutty flavour due to using brown sugar. Use all caster, if you prefer. You will be left with two oranges without zest; use them in a fruit salad.

SERVES 6

For the cake
225g (8oz) baking spread
225g (8oz) self-raising flour
1 level teaspoon baking powder
100g (4oz) caster sugar
100g (4oz) brown sugar
4 eggs
Finely grated zest of 2 oranges

For the butter icing
150g (5oz) butter, softened
300g (10oz) icing sugar, sifted
Finely grated zest of 2 oranges

For the glaze
25g (1oz) caster sugar
Juice of 2 oranges

PREPARE AHEAD
The cake is best made on the day but will keep in the fridge for up to 2 days.

FREEZE
It freezes well un-iced or filled.

Preheat the oven to 180°C/160°C fan/Gas 4. You will need two 20cm (8in) loose-bottomed sandwich tins, greased and base-lined.

Measure all the cake ingredients into a large bowl (reserve a little orange zest for decoration) and beat with a wooden spoon or electric hand mixer until mixed and smooth.

Divide evenly between the two tins. Bake for 20–25 minutes or until well risen, lightly golden and shrinking away from the sides of the tins. After 5 minutes, remove from the tins and leave to cool.

To make the icing, measure the butter and icing sugar into a bowl and mix with an electric hand mixer until light and fluffy. Stir in the orange zest.

Remove the paper from the cakes. Sit one cake upside down on a plate. Make the glaze: measure the caster sugar and orange juice into a saucepan, stir over a low heat until the sugar has dissolved. Boil until reduced by half and then brush half on the upside-down cake, using a pastry brush.

Spread half the butter icing over the glazed cake. Sit the other cake on top, brush with the remaining glaze and then spread with the remaining butter icing. Scatter with the reserved orange zest.

AGA
Bake on the grid shelf on the floor of the roasting oven with the cold sheet on the second set of runners for about 25 minutes. Watch carefully: if it gets too dark, replace the cold sheet above the cake with another cold one or cover the cake with foil.

Sultana & Parmesan Walnut Rolls

These rolls are similar to the Italian olive and cheese rolls in First Courses (see page 22) but the sweet, salty and nutty flavour combination here makes them excellent for afternoon tea. Serve these rolls simply with good butter.

MAKES 12

500g (1lb 2oz) strong white flour
1 × 7g packet fast-action dried yeast
350ml (12fl oz) warm water
4 tablespoon olive oil
2 teaspoons salt
100g (4oz) Parmesan, grated
100g (4oz) sultanas
50g (2oz) walnuts, chopped
1 egg, beaten, to glaze

PREPARE AHEAD
Seal the cooked, cooled rolls inside a plastic bag and keep for up to 24 hours in the fridge. Refresh by sprinkling the rolls with a little water and reheating in a preheated oven at 180°C/160°C fan/Gas 4 for 5–8 minutes.

FREEZE
Freeze for up to 3 months.

AGA
Bake on the grid shelf on the floor of the roasting oven for about 15 minutes. If the bases of the rolls are not quite brown, place the baking sheet on the floor of the roasting oven for a further 5 minutes.

Grease a baking tray. Measure the flour into a large bowl, and add the yeast, water, oil and salt. Mix by hand or using a dough hook until the mixture is a pliable dough. Knead slightly to bring together. It is far better to be on the wet and sticky side than dry.

Grease a bowl, add the dough, cover with clingfilm and leave in a warm place to rise for about 2 hours or until doubled in size.

Turn the dough out on to a lightly floured surface and knock back by kneading until smooth (about 5 minutes), then add the cheese, sultanas and walnuts. Continue to knead until the dough is even (about a further 5 minutes).

Divide the mixture into 12 pieces and form into balls. Arrange them on the baking tray, then brush with beaten egg. Seal the tray inside a large plastic bag, trapping a fair amount of air in the bag so it puffs up well above the dough and is not in contact with it. Leave to rise in a warm place for about 30 minutes until the rolls have doubled in size. Preheat the oven to 200°C/180°C fan/Gas 6.

Bake the rolls for 15–20 minutes, or until a good, crusty, golden brown. Cool on a wire rack.

Basic Recipes

Chicken or Game Stock

Follow this recipe with chicken or pheasant carcasses, or other game birds. If will keep in the freezer for up to 6 months or in the fridge for 1 week.

MAKES 2.5 LITRES (4 PINTS)
1.5kg (3lb) carcasses, trimmings or bones,
    cooked or uncooked, from chicken or game
2–3 onions, unpeeled and cut in half
4 litres (7 pints) water
3 carrots, chopped
3 celery sticks, chopped
1 bouquet garni (bay leaves, thyme, parsley)
½ teaspoon black peppercorns

Put the bones into a stockpot with the onions and cook until browned.

Pour in the water and bring to the boil, skimming off any scum that forms on the surface. Add the remaining vegetables, along with the bouquet garni and peppercorns. Half cover with a pan lid and simmer for 2½ –3 hours, or 5 hours if the bones are uncooked.

Strain the contents of the pan into a large bowl, cool, skim, then decant into pots for freezing or for use in a soup or sauce. When cold, scrape the set fat off the surface – much easier than earlier skimming.

Beef Stock

Make sure that all bottles and fruit are chilled well ahead of time. If you do not have orange liqueur, you could use brandy instead.

MAKES 1.75 LITRES (3 PINTS)
2kg (4lb) beef marrow bones, sawn in 6cm
    (2½in) pieces
2–3 onions, coarsely chopped
2–3 carrots, coarsely chopped
2–3 celery sticks, coarsely chopped
4 litres (7 pints) water
1 bouquet garni (bay leaves, thyme, parsley)
½ teaspoon black peppercorns

Preheat the oven to 230°C/210°C fan/Gas 8.

Put the bones in a roasting tin and roast for 30 minutes. Add the chopped vegetables, turn them in the fat from the bones, and roast for a further 30 minutes.

Tip the contents of the roasting tin into a large pan or stockpot and pour in the water. Bring to the boil, skimming off any scum that forms on the surface, then add the herbs and peppercorns. Leave to simmer very gently for 6–8 hours.

Strain the contents of the pan into a large bowl, cool, skim, then decant into pots for freezing, or for use in a soup or sauce. When cold, scrape the set fat off the surface – much easier than earlier skimming.

Passata Sauce

This is an adaptable sauce that can readily be made more garlicky or hotter by adding a dash or two of Tabasco sauce. Passata, a thickish purée of tomatoes, can be bought from supermarkets in cartons, jars or tins.

MAKES ABOUT 600ML (1 PINT)
15g (½oz) butter
1 medium onion, very finely chopped
1 garlic clove, crushed
600ml (1 pint) passata
1–2 teaspoons sugar
Salt and freshly ground black pepper

Melt the butter in a small pan, stir in the onion and garlic, then cover and cook over a low heat for about 20 minutes until softened but not coloured.

Pour in the passata and add the sugar and some salt and pepper to taste. Bring to the boil and continue to cook for 3–4 minutes or until the sauce has reduced and thickened to your liking.

Prepare ahead: The sauce can be made, quickly cooled, then stored in a sealed container in the fridge for up to 2 days.

Freeze: Pour the sauce into a freezer container. Cool, seal and label, then freeze for up to 3 months. Thaw in the fridge for about 3 hours.

Fresh Herb Sauce

This sauce is perfect with salmon or any other hot or cold, poached or grilled fish. It improves in flavour if it is made the day before as this gives the herbs time to develop and infuse the sauce.

SERVES ABOUT 8
2 tablespoons snipped fresh dill
2 tablespoons snipped fresh chives
2 tablespoons torn fresh mint leaves
2 tablespoons small sprigs of fresh parsley
1 x 200g carton full-fat crème fraîche
1 x 200g carton full-fat Greek yoghurt
300ml (10fl oz) light mayonnaise
Salt and freshly ground black pepper
2 teaspoons sugar
Juice of 1 lemon

Put the herbs into a food processor and process for a second or two to chop them. Add the rest of the ingredients and blend to a smooth sauce. If you do not have a processor, simply finely chop the herbs and combine with the rest of the sauce ingredients.

Taste and season with more salt and pepper if necessary, then pour into a serving boat (not silver, it will discolour), cover with clingfilm and chill in the fridge until ready to serve.

Dill Pickle Sauce

Perfect with cold meat and fish.

SERVES 4
1 x 150g carton full-fat Greek yoghurt
3 tablespoons drained Cucumber & Dill Pickle
    (see page 15), coarsely chopped
1 garlic clove, crushed
1 tablespoon chopped fresh parsley
1–2 teaspoons vinegar taken from the dill pickles
Salt and freshly ground black pepper

Combine the first five ingredients in a small bowl, mix and season to taste with salt and pepper. Cover and chill in the fridge for at least 1 hour before serving.

Prepare ahead: The made sauce can be kept covered in the fridge for up to 8 hours.

Minted Yoghurt Sauce

A simple, Greek-inspired sauce to serve with butterflied lamb.

SERVES 4
1 x 150g carton full-fat Greek yoghurt
Grated zest and juice of 1 lemon
1 garlic clove, crushed
3 tablespoons chopped fresh mint
Salt and freshly ground black pepper

Combine the first four ingredients in a small bowl, mix and season to taste with salt and pepper. Cover and chill in the fridge for at least 1 hour before serving.

Prepare ahead: The made sauce can be kept covered in the fridge for up to 8 hours.

Tip: A first-rate quick version is to add just 2 tablespoons of concentrated mint sauce to a 150g carton of Greek yoghurt, stir and serve!

The Store Cupboard

Keep an efficient store cupboard stocked with really useful ingredients that will last a long time. The following ingredients are handy to have and are used most frequently in this book. I'm not suggesting you go out and buy everything in one go, but build up your reserves over time and you'll have the building blocks to rustle up recipes at a moment's notice.

DRIED HERBS & SPICES
Dill
Bay leaves
Rosemary
Sage
Ground spices: coriander, cumin, cardamom, cloves, cinnamon, turmeric, mixed spice, chilli powder, Chinese five-spice, mild paprika, cayenne pepper
Cinnamon sticks
Curry powders: medium curry powder, hot madras, garam masala
Whole nutmeg

SEASONINGS
Black peppercorns
Coarse sea salt
Dark soy sauce
Garlic bulb
Gravy browning
Sauces: sweet chilli dipping sauce, Tabasco, teriyaki, Worcestershire sauce
Stock cubes (beef, chicken, fish and vegetable – go for the softer cubes)

OILS
Olive oil – mild for cooking and extra-virgin for dressings
Also: sesame, sunflower and vegetable oils
Vinegars: balsamic, malt and white wine vinegars

SUGARS
Caster sugar
Runny honey
Demerara sugar
Golden syrup
Granulated sugar
Icing sugar
Light muscovado sugar
Maple syrup

I use granulated sugar for general sweetening; caster sugar, which is finer, for baking; and I have icing sugar, light muscovado and demerara for icing, crunchy toppings and adding a fudgy flavour to cakes and puddings. They all keep for long periods of time, in sealed containers.

Tip: If you find your muscovado sugar becomes a solid block in its bag, put a clean, damp j-cloth in the bag to separate the grains.

TINNED GOODS AND JARS
Anchovies in oil
Apple or redcurrant jelly
Artichoke hearts in oil or water
Black olives in brine
Black-eyed beans
Capers
Chargrilled peppers in oil
Chopped tomatoes and passata
Coconut milk
Condensed full-fat milk
Couscous
Creamed coconut
Dijon mustard
Flageolet beans
Fruit jams (for sandwiching cakes, glazing tarts or basting ham)
Horseradish sauce
Mango chutney
Mint jelly
Mustard powder
Raspberry jelly
Red kidney beans
Red Thai curry paste
Sardines in oil
Semolina
Stem ginger in syrup
Sun-dried tomato paste
Sweetcorn
Thick-cut marmalade
Tinned fruit (pears, apricots, mandarin oranges, nectarine and black cherries are all useful)
Tuna in oil
Wholegrain mustard

PASTA AND NOODLES
Fusilli
Lasagne
Long-grain rice
Medium Chinese egg noodles
Pappardelle
Penne
Spaghetti

BAKING
Almond extract
Baking powder
Belgian white chocolate
Cocoa powder
Digestive biscuits
Evaporated milk
Fast-action dried yeast
Flaked almonds
Ginger biscuits
Good-quality dark chocolate (40 per cent cocoa solids)
Ground almonds
Mixed fruit (candied peel)
Powdered gelatine
Short-grain rice (for puddings)
Sultanas
Vanilla extract

FLOURS
Cornflour
Plain flour
Self-raising flour
Strong white bread flour
Wholemeal flour

I add a little baking powder with self-raising flour when baking, but never too much; otherwise your cake will rise in the oven but sink as it cools. Check the sell-by dates on flour and baking powder; they go off over time and lose their potency.

Using Your Freezer

I don't cook specifically for the freezer anymore, but if I am making something like mince, I'll still make double and freeze half. Most things freeze well – cooked or raw – so it pays to make the most of your freezer.

All fats, apart from oil, can be frozen so freeze extra butter, high-fat cheeses and milk for when stocks are low.

The number of people staying with us can vary so drastically these days – I never know how much milk we are going to need so I always keep a pint or two in the freezer, just in case. It freezes very well; just leave it to defrost thoroughly. The waters will defrost before the fats so give it a shake to combine before using. I also freeze fruit juice. The fat content of cream varies and some lower-fat creams cannot be frozen. However, whipping cream (35 per cent fat), double cream (48 per cent fat) and clotted cream (55 per cent fat) can all be frozen.

Eggs can be frozen, too, as long as they are separated first – you can't freeze whole eggs in their shells or when cooked, but you can freeze both egg yolks and egg whites for up to 6 months.

Fish, poultry and meat are often more economical bought in larger batches – divide the packets up into freezer bags and store the surplus in your freezer for up to 6 months.

Bread and cakes keep in the freezer for up to 3 months – keeping sliced bread in the freezer is handy if you're cooking for one or two, you can just take slices as you need, when you need it. Raw bread dough and pastry that hasn't been frozen before (check ready-made pastry packets) can be frozen for up to 6 months, too.

I keep home-baked biscuits and cut cookie dough in the freezer ready to be refreshed in the oven or quickly baked when needed.

'Open freeze' iced cakes, before wrapping them in freezer bags or sealing them into freezer boxes. Open freezing means putting them into the freezer on a baking tray so that cake becomes firm before wrapping it – this will prevent the icing being damaged.

Home-made ice cream is not difficult to make, so why not add some to your freezer for a quick weeknight dessert? Sandwich scoops of your ice cream between home-made biscuits, and you've got a quick family dessert.

You can buy lots of very good stock cubes and ready-made fresh stocks, but there are some recipes for stock in this book to try. They can be frozen for up to 6 months – thaw at room temperature before using in soups, stocks and risottos.

I also freeze fresh ginger – much better than letting it become a dried-out nugget in the fridge or cupboard. And I freeze nuts (high in fat) to prevent them going stale. They will keep in the freezer for up to 3 months, as will other tougher herbs, such as bay leaves.

Foods that contain too much water can't be frozen. Salad ingredients don't freeze, nor do softer herbs such as parsley and basil. You can chop them and mix with some butter to freeze: form a sausage-shaped roll of the herbed butter and chill. Then chop into thin pieces and put into a freezer bag. Use the herby butter on steaks.

Cooked vegetables don't freeze well for the same reason, but fresh, uncooked vegetables and fruit do freeze. They might lose their firmness when defrosted, but they will still taste good.

Pies with potato toppings don't freeze well though you may find it useful to freeze shepherd's pie or cottage pie – just make the potato topping a little stiffer, adding butter instead of milk.

Useful things to have in your fridge and freezer, which are used most often in this book:

Fridge
Sauces and flavouring
Fresh pesto
Tomato purée

DAIRY
Baking spread
Cheddar cheese
Double cream or whipping cream
Full-fat cream cheese
Full-fat Greek yoghurt, plain natural yoghurt or full-fat crème fraîche
Mayonnaise
Parmesan or Pecorino
Unsalted butter

FRUIT
Lemons
Limes

FRESH HERBS
Bay leaves
Basil (a useful fresh herb, but keep this out of the fridge)
Dill
Parsley sprigs
Thyme

Bacon – streaky or rashers,
smoked or unsmoked

Freezer
Carton of semi-skimmed milk
Blackberries
Chestnuts
Herb cheese toasts (page 216)
Mixed seafood
Peas and broad beans
Raspberries
Raw prawns
Ready-roll puff pastry
Ready-made filo pastry
Ready-made shortcrust pastry
Sliced loaf
Spinach
Vanilla ice cream

Label everything – what it is and
when it was frozen – so you can
keep track of your supplies.

When food is taken straight from
the fridge to be cooked, remember
to allow extra time for it to heat
through. With meats it is best to
allow them to come up to room
temperature before cooking.

Useful Equipment

*The following items
are used most often in this book:*

DISHES AND BOWLS
1-litre (2-pint) pudding basin
1.5-litre (2½-pint) ovenproof dish
2-litre (3½-pint) pie dish
2.5-litre (4-pint) ovenproof dish
3-litre (5-pint) ovenproof dish
a shallow, rectangular pie dish,
    28 x 23cm, 1.5-litre (11 x 9in,
    2½-pint) capacity
oval gratin dish (about 28cm
    /11in long)
Shallow, flameproof dish (about
    30 x 20 x 6cm/12 x 8 x 2½in)

TINS
12-hole mini muffin tin
2 x 20cm (8in) round sandwich tins
2 x 23cm (9in) sandwich tins
2 x deep 23cm (9in) round, loose-
    bottomed or springform tins
20cm (8in) round springform tin
23 x 11.5cm (9 x 4½in) non-stick
    loaf tin
28cm (11in) fluted loose-
    bottomed tin
33 x 23cm (13 x 9in) large
    Swiss roll tin
4-hole Yorkshire pudding tin
8 x metal dariole moulds
Baking tray (ideally 2 trays) or
    heavy baking sheet
Large roasting tin with a
    wire rack

If you have only one baking tray,
cool it under cold running water
before cooking another batch. It's
useful to have 2 baking trays – it
will save you time.

CUTTERS
3.5cm (1¼in) plain cutter
8 x 7cm (3in) cooking rings

PANS
A large wok
Frying pan
Grill pan
Large deep pan
Large saucepan
Medium saucepan
Omelette pan

It's worth investing in decent
pans that are suitable for the
type of hob that you have.

TOOLS
6- or 8-point star nozzle
6 small ramekins
Aluminium foil
Baking parchment
Clingfilm
Colander
Food processor
Freezer bags (large and small)

Grater with coarse and fine holes
Hand-held electric whisk
Heatproof measuring jug
Kitchen paper
Large bowl
Metric spoons: tablespoon,
    teaspoon, dessertspoon,
    serving spoons
Palette knife
Piping bags
Plain 1cm nozzle
Sharp kitchen scissors
Sharp knives (large and small)
Sieve
Wooden cocktail skewers
Wooden spoons

Health & Safety

*I don't want to go into too much
detail about all the hazards in the
kitchen! Common sense is key
when using hot ovens, sharp
knifes and kitchen equipment.
I've noted the key points to
remember in the Cook's Notes
(page 9), but here is a little bit
of extra information.*

Dishwashers, with their high
temperatures, are really helpful
at keeping germs at bay, but it's
still good practice to have
separate chopping boards for
cooked and uncooked meats.
This will ensure you avoid
cross-contamination,
particularly when cutting
something like chicken.

Always wash your hands after
handling raw meat, fish and eggs.
I was asked once whether I
washed eggs before use, because
they often come straight from the
hen coop. I have to admit that I
don't because the eggs are usually
going into something that will be
cooked or boiled, killing any

germs. However, I wash my hands once I've finished baking.

Never leave anything out in the kitchen overnight. Leave hot food to go cold and then cover and refrigerate as quickly as possible. Large batches of food are likely to go off more quickly, so if you have made something for a crowd, cool it as quickly as possible – I dip the saucepan into cold water to cool it quickly before transferring the contents into a suitable container, then covering it and putting it straight into the fridge.

Leftover rice can be a little tricky, because of a bacteria found in all cereals that can cause upset stomachs. If you have leftover rice, be particularly careful about cooling and refrigerating it as quickly as possible and, as with all reheated food, make sure it is 'piping hot' before eating it.

Put cooked dishes and foods to be eaten raw on the higher shelves in your fridge and any raw meat and fish nearer the bottom so avoid cross-contamination.

Menu Planning

Make as much ahead of the occasion as you can, and freeze it. Don't put a menu together that all has to be cooked at the last minute – choose a mixture of make-ahead dishes, quick no-cook dishes and then a couple of recipes that need to be cooked just before serving. And if it's your main course that needs some final cooking, make sure there is nothing left to be done on the starters and dessert. I stack plated first courses and chilled puds in the fridge so that they are ready to go.

You might also find it easier to present courses on serving platters so that guests can help themselves at the table while you all sit together. Otherwise, you'll spend the whole night as cook rather than host.

It might seem obvious, but, if you choose fish for the first course, don't have a fishy main course as well. If pastry features in the starter, don't serve a tart for dessert. Cheese shouldn't appear in both savoury courses, particularly if you want to offer a cheeseboard as well.

Think about texture – a smooth creamy soup, followed by a crunchy salad works well. A creamy soup, followed by a savoury mousse, then a creamy pudding is not be a good idea! Choose a mixture of colours as well as textures, so your food is a feast for the eyes as well.

I would usually serve two seasonal vegetables along with potatoes at a dinner party, to give people choice. And I would have two dessert options when feeding a large group too – one chocolatey and one fruity pud works well, or one light and one rich option. And ideally your guests will be hungry after the first course, so aim for small portions – people can go back for seconds.

Feeding a Crowd

It's always difficult to think in terms of exact quantities when cooking for a crowd. The more people you have, often the less they will eat. Although, four teenagers can also consume

enough for 10 people. The time of day is a crucial factor – at an afterwork party, guests might be starving, but appetites might be a little jaded post-Christmas.

The lists below offer some general guidelines for estimating food and drink quantities for different occasions. See also page 128 for ideas for open sandwiches and page 234 for afternoon tea sandwich ideas, which can be scaled up for large numbers.

SANDWICHES
1 large sandwich loaf, thin-cut, about 24 slices

1 large sandwich loaf, medium-cut, about 20 slices

1 large sandwich loaf, thick-cut, about 16 slices

1 long baguette, about 20 slices

Butter: about 100g per large sandwich loaf or 12 bread rolls (always have it soft and spreadable – it goes further!)

SANDWICH FILLINGS
The following fillings are each enough to make 10 sandwiches, using one large medium-cut loaf, or 12–13 sandwiches using a thinly sliced loaf:

Cheese & chutney: 300g (11oz) grated cheese, plus 4 tablespoons of chutney.

Salmon: 450g (1lb) tinned salmon, drained and flaked, then mixed with mayonnaise.

Egg: 6 hard-boiled eggs, chopped and bound with mayonnaise.

Meat: 350g (12oz) thinly sliced meat with salad

Cucumber: 1, thinly sliced.

LIQUIDS

Champagne: 8 glasses per bottle
Cream: 600ml (1 pint) per about
12 portions
Milk for coffee: 900ml (1½ pint)
per 20 cups
Milk for tea: 600ml (1 pint) per
20 cups
Wine: 6 glasses per bottle

SAVOURY DISHES PER PERSON (RAW WEIGHTS)

Joint with bone: 175–225g
(6–8oz)
Joint without bone: 100–175g
(4–6oz)
Meat for casseroles: 175g (6oz)
Pasta, uncooked: 75–100g
(3–4oz)
Rice, uncooked: 40–50g (1½–2oz)
Salmon: 100–125g (4–4½oz)
Soup: 600ml (1 pint) will serve
3 people
Steak: 175g (6oz)

SWEET DISHES PER PERSON

Cakes: a 25cm (10in) sponge will
serve 16 people

Meringues: 6 egg whites and
350g (12oz) caster sugar will
make about 30 small meringues
Raspberries: 75–100g (3–4oz)
Strawberries: 100g (4oz)

NIBBLES

Potato crisps: 25g (1oz)
per person
Salted nuts: 15g (½oz) per person

DRINKS PARTIES & BUFFETS

Drinks parties: 5–6 savoury
items, plus nuts and crisps;
3–4 drinks

Finger buffets: 8–10 items (a
couple of them sweet); 3–4 drinks

Fork buffet: 1 first course, 1 main
course with accompaniments
(vegetables, salads, etc), and
2 desserts and/or cheese.

There is some more information
on sandwich-making on page 253
and on the same page there is a
list offering some general
guidelines for various scenarios.

Presentation

Arrange food at buffet-style
dinners so that plates are the
first thing people collect, followed
by food (first courses through
to puddings) and then cutlery
and napkins.

Depending on numbers, I suggest
offering a couple of starters, two
or three main courses, both hot
and cold, a large bowl of salad
and a couple of vegetables.

Choose food that is easy to eat
standing up and that offer
complementary textures.

If you are short of wine glasses,
it is a good idea to tie a label
around the stems of the glasses
with each guest's name. Then
everyone can then keep it for the
evening, and other guests can
read their names.

Index